COOL WOMEN

Edited by Pam Nelson
Written by Dawn Chipman
Mari Florence
Naomi Wax
Designed by Amy Inouye

SCHOLASTIC INC.
New York Toronto London Auckland Sydney
Mexico City New Delhi Hong Kong

ISBN 0-439-26705-6

Copyright © 1998 by Girl Press.
All rights reserved.
Published by Scholastic Inc., 555 Broadway, New York, NY 10012,
by arrangement with Girl Press Publishing.
SCHOLASTIC and associated logos are trademarks and/or
registered trademarks of Scholastic Inc.

12 11 10 9 8 7 6 5 4 3 2 1   1 2 3 4 5 6/0

Printed in the U.S.A.   14

First Scholastic printing, January 2001

This book is not about heroine worship—on the contrary, it's about taking our heroines down from their pedestals where we can get a good, hard look at them. Because only there, at eye level, can we see what's truly inspiring, even startling, about their stories—that they're not all that different from our own.

Because with the exception of a few fictional characters, what made each of these women glorious was not her flawlessness, but her humanity. Look into the eyes of their pictures—the courage that stares back at you is not about fearlessness, it's about fears that have been overcome, mistakes that have been made, and a lives that have been lived for the sheer adventure of it.

So, sure, this book is about great stories from the past, but more importantly it's about stories still to come. Cool Women aims for that moment of recognition, that EUREKA that comes when a girl or woman finds the story that sings to her. That instant is about more than inspiration, or even transformation—that instant is about takeoff.

*I have seen strange things,
and they color the mind.*
—Gertrude Bell

Contents

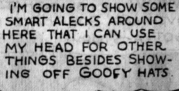

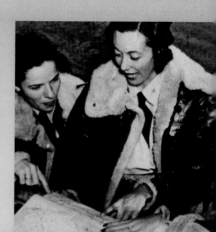

AMAZONS

FIERCE, FREE, AND FEROCIOUS—

AMAZONS WERE THE WARRIOR QUEENS OF ANCIENT MYTHOLOGY.

They ruled their corner of the world in all-female tribes, controlling their land and scaring the daylights out of any man who tried to interfere.

The original stories of Amazons come from Greek mythology—although there now is evidence that some version of this civilization really *did* exist. In any case, the very idea of Amazon warriors apparently had the Greeks scared silly. Greek authors wrote endlessly about the fierceness of these fighting women, and their stories are filled with images of ruthless Amazons raiding and pillaging their way through the ancient world.

According to the Greeks, these tribes of warrior women lived around the Black Sea, and terrified just about anybody who came near their turf. The Amazons didn't mind pairing up with men from other cultures from time to time, but they had no interest in keeping them around. Nor did they mind having children: but true to the Amazon way, they only kept the girls, and sent the boys off to live with their fathers. The girls were trained to be true Amazons, and learned how to hunt, ride a horse, and, of course, do battle with the best of the warriors.

One legend even has it that the only way for a girl to prove herself as a full-fledged Amazon was to kill her first enemy in battle.

Hey—we never said they were saints.

Myth or Not-So-Myth?

For the most part, the Amazon written about by the Greek are considered pure fiction—a part of mythological lore like Athen and Zeus. But recent discoveries archeologists have suggested tha some version of these tribes really d exist. New digs are uncovering th graves of women who were burie with their weapons, suggesting th these "Amazons" were the dominan warriors in their society. Interesting there is even evidence that the me took charge of the more domest duties, like weaving, childcare, an cooking.

IS XENA AN AMAZON?

OF COURSE! Xena (played by Lucy Lawless on T.V.) is the ultimate Amazon. The show may not be true to the historical record, but Xena's warrior ways and independent lifestyle are straight out of the Amazon rulebook. For one thing, Xena is an expert in the ways of war and fierce in the martial arts. (Her favorite weapon is the "chakram"—kind of a fearsome boomerang that wreaks havoc on olden-day bad guys.) Xena's attitude toward men is also pure Amazon—she's willing to engage in an occasional flirtation, but has no interest in settling down. Xena prefers to hang with her Amazon sisters to get the job done.

The **AMAZON RIVER** was, according to legend, named for the armies of fighting women encountered by the Spaniards while exploring South America.

Amazons, Amazons Everywhere

But the Greeks don't have a monopoly on the Amazon tall tale. Stories of warring female tribes pop up in narratives from all over the world. In Chinese mythology, writers described "the woman's kingdom," referring to a strange and abundant land where women ruled alone. Indian lore also refers to the *rhackshasis*—female warriors ruled by other women.

For real-live Amazons, you should turn to South America in your history books. According to the Spanish explorers who first "discovered" the New World, warring women showed up just about everywhere they went.

In Chile, the Spanish conquistadors told stories of Gaboimilla (Indian translation: "Heaven of Gold"), who was called the Queen of the Amazons in that region. Another explorer named Orellana complained of being attacked by an all-female army in Venezuela, and conquistador Pizarro wrote of the women warriors who killed many of his men during his travels throughout South America. In Peru, the land of the "puna" is well documented as a civilization of female tribes who retreated to the high plateaus of their land. (The puna regions today are still considered "women-only" territory.)

Did They Really Have to Cut One Off?

The most notorious custom of the mythic Amazons was having one breast removed to improve their aim with a bow and arrow. Thankfully, that particular myth is not thought to be based in fact.

Today, the term "Amazon" is often used to describe any strong or powerful woman.

Josephine Baker

THINK JOSEPHINE BAKER AND YOU THINK GLAMOUR—

Wild, dangerous kind of glamour that makes you want to run off to Paris and do something intoxicating and reckless. Maybe you'd scandalize Parisian nightclubs, or work for the French Resistance. In fact, checking those two tasks off your "to-do" list would only give you a glimpse of what it was like to walk in Josephine's sequined, stiletto heels.

Not only did Josephine Baker break all the rules about feminine independence, but she exploded every idea about what a black woman could be by simply and elegantly refusing to recognize them. She was just too busy basking in international acclaim, entertaining dashing suitors, and even helping the French underground fight the Nazis.

WHO HAD TIME FOR STEREOTYPES?

LE JAZZ HOT

JOSEPHINE'S SPECTACULAR SUCCESS WAS EVEN MORE REMARKABLE GIVEN HER DESTITUTE BEGINNINGS. SHE WAS BORN IN THE POOREST SECTION OF ST. LOUIS, LIVED IN CARDBOARD BOXES, AND RUMMAGED FOR FOOD IN THE STREETS. SHE WAITRESSED AT A NIGHTCLUB WHEN SHE WAS THIRTEEN, AND EVENTUALLY LANDED A JOB AS A DANCER WITH A MINSTREL BAND. SHE WENT TO PARIS WITH THE "REVUE NEGRE" IN 1925, AND, ALTHOUGH THE SHOW FAILED, THE FRENCH WERE FASCINATED BY JOSEPHINE'S STYLE—THE ORIGINAL **LE JAZZ HOT.**

4

> "Tall, coffee skin, ebony eyes, legs of paradise, a smile to end all smiles."
> —Pablo Picasso

Josephine's "to-do" list might have looked something like this →

1. Get fancy job dancing with ~~chorus line in Chicago~~ ~~with Ziegfield Follies in New York~~ racy nightclubs in Paris! ✓

2. Be international ~~cabaret star~~
   Film star — Zou-Zou
   — Princess Tam-Tam

3. Become toast of Paris ✓
4. Try daring spy work : German occupation ✓
   French Air Force ✓
   French Resistance ✓

(circled) Walk leopard down Champs-Elysee

5. Win ~~Medal of Resistance~~ ~~French Legion of Honor~~
6. Entertain dashing suitors. Marry the lucky ones.
   ~~Willie~~
   ~~Willie 2~~
   ~~Jean~~
   Joe
   ~~Robert~~

7. Live in exotic locales: Paris
   ~~Morocco~~
   ~~Back to Paris~~ ✓
8. Stateside: Weigh in on civil rights nightmare ✓
   '63 March on Washington ✓

The French love affair with Josephine lasted for half a century, as she developed from a minor celebrity into a full-fledged national heroine after her work for the French Resistance in World War II. She was sickened by the treatment of blacks in the United States and boycotted America for the majority of her career. She returned to her homeland as an important spokesperson during the civil rights "March on Washington" in 1963, but would always consider Paris her real home. Her death in 1975 triggered an unprecedented national mourning, and she was given an elaborate state funeral—the first ever for a non-native French citizen.

> "Her magnificent dark body, a new model to the French, proved for the first time that black was beautiful."
> —Janet Flanner
> *New Yorker* correspondent

See Janet Flanner's profile at page 34

Lucille Ball

ONE OF THE MOST POWERFUL personalities in the world of television, Lucille Ball virtually defined an era of entertainment. Along the way, she established herself as a brilliant comedienne, built a small Hollywood empire, and even shot down a few antiquated notions about women. Of course, we hardly noticed any of that because we were too busy laughing. Maybe that's why, fifty years later,

we still love Lucy.

Don't let the clowning fool you—

Lucy was also one of the smartest women in the entertainment industry. She and her husband, Desi Arnaz, built their own entertainment empire (Desilu Productions) during a time when most entertainers were chained to the studio or network systems.

A FEMININE FACE ON COMEDY

One of the most important things that Lucy showed us was that women could be funny and attractive all at once— a groundbreaking concept for the day. This was particularly admirable given that Lucy was beautiful enough to be a conventional film star, and, in fact had become a Hollywood movie sensation as "Queen of the B-Movies." But she shrugged off the persona of a cool beauty, instead reveling in the chance to get a laugh. She was never afraid to look foolish, silly, or even ugly for the sake of a good gag and her public loved her for it. By proving this formula, she paved the way for generations of funny women to come. Think of Carol Burnett, Roseanne, Gilda Radner, and Candice Bergen—they all owe at least a part of their success to the amazing Lucy.

Lucy's brand of comedy could sometimes get a little rough. In the famous "candy factory" episode, the "fake" slapping fight she had with a fellow candy-wrapper actually involved a couple of pretty good whacks.

And in an Italian grape-stomping scene in which a similar tussle was staged, Lucy later said that she was afraid she was going to drown in the vat of grape juice when the other actress became a bit too enthusiastic.

The Lucy Phenomenon

When I Love Lucy aired on Monday nights, the country came to virtual standstill to watch it. More than ten million T.V. sets were tuned in to the show on those nights (there were only fifteen million in the U.S. at the time).

In 1952, when presidential candidate Adlai Stevenson interrupted the show for a campaign pitch, he was deluged by angry viewers. (One woman wrote "I love Lucy. I like Ike. Drop dead.") The department store Marshall Field's moved its evening shopping hours from Monday to Thursday, because business was so bad on that night. (They put up a sign saying "We love Lucy, too.") More people watched the show that announced Little Ricky's birth in 1953 than watched the swearing in of Eisenhower as the new president. In fact, the "Lucy Goes to the Hospital" episode drew a 92 percent share and a 71.1 Nielsen rating—a record which stood for decades.

Lucy WAS BORN IN JAMESTOWN, NEW YORK, ON AUGUST 6, 1911. She was *born* to be an entertainer, and would often herd her neighborhood friends into impromptu plays and productions. She was amazingly ambitious from an early age, and took off for New York City to find stardom when she was only fifteen years old.

HARD KNOCKS AND HARD WORK best define Lucy's road to success. Her early experience in show business would have turned back all but the most stubborn of personalities. Her first acting school coach recommended that she find a different career, and she was fired from her first four chorus-line jobs. Lucy's first break came when she landed a chorus girl role in a movie called *Roman Scandals*. She headed to Hollywood, where she began to get other small movie roles, and eventually worked her way up the ladder to success.

BUT EVEN AS THE STAR OF HER OWN SHOW, she is remembered as being the hardest working person on the set. Lucy's brand of comedy was highly energetic, and demanded a great deal of physical stamina. During her pregnancy, her fellow actors remember Lucy leaving the set for a few minutes to throw up, then coming right back to start again. No complaints.

THAT KIND OF ENERGY DEFINED HER ENTIRE LIFE. She ran production companies (Lucille Ball Productions came after Desilu), created more classic television (including *The Lucy Show* and *Here's Lucy*), raised two children (Lucie Arnaz and Desi Arnaz, IV), starred on Broadway, and acted in a total of eighty movies. She won four Emmy Awards, a Lifetime Achievement Citation from the Kennedy Center, and a Presidential Medal of Freedom. When she died in 1989, she left behind a public that revered her as an American icon. Her most important legacy, of course, is the classic T.V. and movie moments that she created. Our Lucy might appreciate being missed, but—let's face it—she would most like the fact she can still make us laugh.

BARNSTORMING
Baseball Girls

The Muskegon LASSIES

CITY OF MUSKEGON MICHIGAN

1947 YEAR BOOK   25¢

DON'T get in the way of a GIRL with BASEBALL in her BLOOD. Since the game was founded, women have endured anything to play the game they LOVE. They've worn stupid skirts, risked broken bones, and endured the worst kind of ridicule for the chance to get on to the field. Why? Even though the teams were usually reserved for men, the sheer rush of playing the game wasn't. Women didn't play to prove a point, they played because they loved it.

Since baseball was invented in 1846, women have been angling to get their chance on the field. This was no easy task in this era, as they usually had to haul about thirty pounds of extra clothes along with them. Imagine sprinting the bases in a long dress and stockings and you've got a pretty good idea of what these women were willing to do. Although they clearly loved the sport, any organized "girl" games were looked on as a kind of sideshow. Remember—these were the days when a sporting woman was the rough equivalent of a singing frog, at least to many of the male onlookers.

Female baseball players endured this freak-show treatment for decades, until the barnstorming teams of the 1930s emerged on the scene. These teams (including the "House of David" on which Babe Didrikson played) were usually sponsored by a company who wanted to gain attention from their novelty appeal.

And then came a league of their own. In 1944, women were finally given the chance to play serious organized ball, when the AAGPBL (the All-American Girl's Professional Baseball League) was formed by Phil Wrigley. The league was conceived as a way to boost morale during World War II, when many fans were afraid the men's league would be shut down because of the draft.

Once again, the owners made it clear to the female ball players that their appearance was more important than their athletic skills. Their uniforms incorporated skirts so they would appear more "feminine"—never mind that they tore

Babe Didrikson played on the barnstorming "House of David" team. See her separate profile.

8

...p their legs with every base slide. Makeup was required on the field, and slacks were never allowed "on the street." The women endured this ridiculous treatment for a chance to play the game they loved, and the fans responded in kind. By 1948, the league was drawing more than one million fans per year to its various games around the Midwest.

Despite Wrigley's loss of enthusiasm for the league (he sold it after only two seasons), it operated for eleven years and the number of teams grew from four to ten. Before the AAGPBL was disbanded in 1954, more than six hundred women had the opportunity to play in the "big leagues."

Women gone from the field? Don't count on it. The spirit of teams like the Milwaukee Chicks and Rockford Peaches is still going strong. Girls and women everywhere are playing baseball and softball by the millions, because, as it turns out, the thrill of landing a solid hit, or sliding safe into third has nothing to do with being a boy. Besides, a real baseball girl never listens to the people who tell her to stay on the sidelines, or to go back to her dolls. A real baseball girl hears only one thing, and it's pure music to her ears—

PLAY BALL!

The teams had names like the Rockford Peaches, the Racine Belles, Fort Wayne Daisies, Muskegon Lassies, and Milwaukee Chicks.

The AAGPBL Charm School Guide

The team owners were so nervous about their players being perceived as masculine that they developed a "charm school guide" for the league.

A few choice excerpts:

HAIR—The inner charm . . . can suffer beneath a sloppy or stringy coiffure . . .

BODY—Superfluous hair on arms or legs can be easily removed . . .

CLOTHES—On the field, there is a real "lift" noticeable in the smartly turned out and neatly arrayed aggregation; slacks are not permitted for street wear . . .

WHO THROWS LIKE A GIRL?

Pitcher Jackie Mitchell proved what a woman could do on the pitching mound when she struck out both Babe Ruth and Lou Gehrig in an exhibition game in 1931.

Are you a baseball girl??

Check out these spots for more info . . .

• National Baseball Hall of Fame— "Women in Baseball" exhibit • www.baseballhalloffame.org

• American Women's Baseball League • www.womenplayingbaseball.com

• Ladies League Baseball • www.ladiesleaguebaseball.com

• *A League of Their Own* (1992) — directed by Penny Marshall

Gertrude Bell

Gertrude Bell with Winston Churchill (left of her)

World traveler to exotic lands, master politician, archaeologist, and poet, Gertrude Bell was more than a woman, she was an action movie on camel-back. On any given day during her lifetime, when most women were bound to domestic duties, Gertrude would likely be found trekking across the desert by horse or camel, in full Victorian garb. She had a passion for exploration and a talent for diplomacy that was extraordinary by any day's standards. That's the reason she was hailed as the "Uncrowned Queen of Arabia."

The GLAMOUR of TRAVEL

Although true to her Victorian background, Gertrude was the heartiest and most resourceful of travelers. She spent many days riding in the searing heat, covered with dust, and under constant threat of attack from roving Arab tribes. She talked her way out of many a dangerous spot by using her natural diplomatic skills.

Gertrude was good friends with the famous "Lawrence of Arabia" (T. E. Lawrence), and many believe that she was actually the brains behind his brawn. No surprise.

"You will find me a savage, for I have seen strange things, and they colour the mind."

—G.B. in a letter to home in 1914

Gertrude had a huge impact on the redrawn borders of the Middle East after World War I, and especially on the establishment of the country of Iraq.

...trude was highly praised
...her political skills, but
...e was often annoyed at
...e sexist implication behind
...e acclaim. She commented
...one report: "The general
...e . . . seems to be that
...most remarkable that a
...g should be able to stand
...on its hind legs—i.e.,
...emale write a . . . paper."

the DESERT QUEEN

Gertrude Bell was born in
Middlesbrough, England, into
a life of relative wealth and comfort,
although her childhood was saddened
by the death of her mother when she was
only four. Her father remarried when she was
eight, and her stepmother, Florence Olliffe,
had an important and positive impact on her childhood.
Florence encouraged a free-thinking and adventurous attitude
toward life, and "Gertie" took her advice to heart. Gertrude also adored
her father, Hugh Bell, who often told her that "obstacles are made to be
overcome." Although Gertrude was raised during a constrictive time for women,
her family was unusually supportive of her right to education and independence.
She was allowed to attend Oxford (one of the only two colleges to allow women
at the time), and she flourished in every way. Her archaeological studies led her to the Middle
East, which she found exhausting, strenuous, and intoxicating. Gertrude had found her home.
In the course of her many archaeological digs and travels, she gradually became an expert on
northern and central Arabia. She was a skilled linguist, and well-versed in the complex customs of the various regional Arabic tribes. Her talents were first recognized by the British government during World War I, when
she was asked to gather information for the British intelligence service.
After the war, her unmatched authority on the Middle East was officially recognized when she was appointed chief
political officer to the transitional British government in Iraq. During her time in this and other government positions, Gertrude
exerted more power over the politics of the Middle East than any other single individual. Kings, tribal leaders, and heads of state called
on her. Any Arab or British leader in search of advice or influence in the area eventually came to her door.
Gertrude was the ultimate renaissance woman—aside from her formidable political skills, she was an accomplished writer, photographer, and curator of ancient artifacts. But despite her adventures and influence, we know very little about her experiences. Maybe
someday, as with her friend Lawrence, we'll see a movie about her life—the story of Gertrude Bell, better known as

Gertrude of Arabia.

*And we don't even
have room to tell you
about Gertrude's
mountain-climbing
exploits.*

Do YOU have a TRAVEL BUG for Exotic Lands??

• **Check into the foreign exchange program at your school**

• **Learn a foreign language!**

• **And to read more about Gertrude's life, pick up**
  Desert Queen, **by Janet Wallach (Bantam Doubleday, 1996)**

BLUES DIVAS

*H*earing Bessie Smith sing the blues was like getting hit full-on by a truckload of feminine power. Audiences were stunned by the raw emotion of her performances, and it turned her into one of the most successful singers of the century. Sure we still love Janis Joplin and Tina Turner, but we can't forget that women like Bessie Smith showed us how to rock.

"I knew that she was a no-nonsense kind of chick."
— *Etta James*

Bessie Smith

*S*trong female performers ruled the "Roaring 20s," and while Mae West was tearing up the silver screen, women like **Bessie Smith** were packing the nightclubs. She was quickly nicknamed the "Empress of the Blues," because no one seemed to have claimed this new genre of music with quite the same authority as Bessie.

As luck would have it, Bessie got her start when she was discovered by another blues legend, **Ma Rainey,** with whom she traveled in a revue during her early career. Bessie's take-no-prisoners style was a hit wherever they went, and she soon landed a recording contract.

Thus began the career of one of the most successful entertainers of the decade. Commanding the amazing sum of $1,500 per week, Bessie Smith became the highest paid black entertainer of the 1920s.

One of the coolest things about Bessie—and all of the other blues divas (**Etta James, Ida Cox, Bertha Hill,** to name a few)— was their new, defiant image of female beauty. A woman could be big and brassy, outspoken and brash, and use it all to get her man. These women created a culture that had no patience for skinny, demure girls who were too silly to speak their mind.

WHEN Janis Joplin discovered that Bessie Smith was buried in an unmarked grave, she paid for a headstone to be placed at the site.

Memphis Minnie had been one of the music world's greatest performers, but she was also buried in an unmarked grave when she died in 1973. This unfitting close to her life was resolved more than two decades later when a group of contemporary musicians, including Bonnie Raitt and John Fogerty, honored Minnie's memory (as well as other greats like Robert Johnson and Sonny Boy Williamson) by having a grave marker erected in their honor.

Memphis Minnie

If you wanted to see a woman play the living daylights out of a blues guitar, you would have headed South. There, on Memphis' famous Beale Street, you would have found **Memphis Minnie**— one of the most influential musicians in all of blues history. Minnie was at the center of the famous thoroughfare's blues scene, and indeed was largely responsible for putting it on the map in the first place. Minnie and the other artists there were performing and refining the new music medium, and have been credited by many with giving birth to blues.

Memphis Minnie (actually born Lizzie Douglas), began her career as a musician early, when she learned to play the banjo at the age of seven. She grew up in the cotton fields of Mississippi, the eldest of thirteen children, and it wasn't long before she had run away to join the Ringling Brothers Circus. There, she learned the art of showmanship and honed her guitar-playing skills as part of the instrumental back-up for the performers. She eventually made her way to Beale Street, where she could earn a living with her guitar.

Minnie was a highly accomplished guitar player, responsible for creating intricate performances for two guitars, as well for developing her own unique slide guitar riffs. If you had walked into one of the Beale Street nightclubs during the 1920s, chances are you would have found Minnie facing off in a guitar contest with another blues legend like Muddy Waters. (Minnie usually won.) The most common—if irksome—comment made about Minnie was that she "played like a man." Memphis Minnie was also a talented and prolific composer, writing more than 150 songs during her lifetime.

he world lost Bessie when she died in a car crash at the young age of thirty-nine. After a dip in her reer, she had planned a comeback, and was on r way to one of her first planned shows. While ssie had lived a hard and fast lifestyle, and many id that she had brought on her own hardship, she ver listened to the outsiders who judged her life. ssie summed up her attitude best in the words of r own song:

"There ain't nothing I can do,
or nothin' I can say,
that folks don't criticize me.
t I'm going to do just as I want to anyway."

Nellie Bly

Daredevil Reporter Deluxe

Nellie Bly would do anything to get her story. Fueled by righteous rage and a rebellious nature, Nellie would take on the world for a good lead. She crashed asylum gates and factory floors, was tossed into prisons and out of countries—all to get at the truth she knew the public deserved to know. Friends, co-workers, and authorities soon learned that there was only one thing to do when Nellie Bly went after a story, and that was to get out of the way.

In just a few of Nellie's undercover exploits, she posed as purse snatcher, a prostitute, a factory worker, and a chorus girl to get the inside scoop.

Born Elizabeth Cochran in 1865, Nellie was aware at an early age of life's crueler side. Everywhere she looked, she saw evidence of an unfair system—children begging on the street, immigrants living in poverty, women struggling without even the most basic of rights. Nellie was struck by the injustice behind these images, and knew that someday she would make a difference.

She got her first chance at the early age of twenty, when she sold stories to a local paper in Pittsburgh about the plight of divorced women—a shocking subject for the day. Public reaction was heated and wildly divergent—some readers called the stories brilliant, others called them indecent—but everyone agreed on one thing: Nellie's stories sold papers. In fact, they sold more papers than anything else in her city. Her editor gave her the pen name "Nellie Bly" (the title of a popular song of the day), and hired her as the paper's first woman reporter. Nellie's career had begun.

Nellie's nose for controversy

Other papers ignored the "hot" issues of the day for fear of offending their readers, but Nellie took them on with a vengeance. She loved the commotion she caused; in truth, Nellie knew that if her story didn't cause an uproar then it probably wasn't worth doing.

Next Stop, New York City.

When Nellie decided that she should work for the biggest paper in the country—the *New York World*—she went after the job with her usual tenacity. Nellie told the editor, Joseph Pulitzer, that she would get him the biggest story of the year by going undercover in the state asylum system. It was a frightening plan—the asylum system of the nineteenth century was little better than a holding pen for society's castoffs, where the inmates were treated more like animals than patients. Nellie knew this, and wanted to write the exposé of the decade.

It would be Nellie Bly's most famous exploit. Nellie moved to a boarding house where no one knew her, faked a breakdown in front of the guests, and, right on cue, was dragged off to the sanitarium. There she spent ten hellish days—the last few trying to convince the guards that she was sane—until the *World* lawyers managed to set her free. Even Nellie was shaken by what she had found inside the asylum gates—patients who were beaten, starved, and forced into hard labor. Some had simple physical ailments like speech defects, but no money for medical treatment.

Her story was a sensation. "Behind Asylum Bars" sold out of stands everywhere. Every paper in the country picked up the story of the daring "girl reporter" and the scandal she had uncovered. Nellie was suddenly the most famous journalist in the country, but even more importantly, the New York asylum system underwent eventual reform, all because of Nellie's amazing undercover work.

Around the World in 72 Days.

In 1889, Nellie set her sites on another life's dream: a trip around the world. But this would be no leisurely trip— Nellie had read *Around the World in Eighty Days*, by Jules Verne, and was determined to break the record of the main character Phineas Fogg. This was a nearly impossible goal for her time—Phineas' trip had been fictional, after all— and international travel was a slow and weary process. Nellie's trip would be an exhausting succession of steamships, railcars, and horse carriages. Nellie ignored the skeptics, and took off.

Nellie Bly's round-the-world adventure brought her instant celebrity. Songs were written about her, clothes were designed after her style (her "travel cap" especially became all the rage), and even her hair style was copied.

Once again, Nellie was the talk of the national media. Papers all over the country tracked her route, and there were "Nellie Bly Guessing Game" contests which bet on her return time. Her trip was grueling and filled with obstacles, but the world was stunned when she made her goal, finishing in seventy-two days. Nellie was an instant celebrity.

But celebrity or not, Nellie never abandoned her muckraking ways. She continued to write about the causes that piqued her passion, and, after a life of firebrand journalism, Nellie died at the young age of fifty-five. Journalism, and the world that it covers, will never be the same.

re you the next Nellie Bly? et the story at these spots:

- ⟩ **Journalism and Women Symposium**
  www.jaws.org

- ⟩ **Reporter.org**
  www.reporter.org

- ⟩ **Association of Women Journalists**
  www.awjchicago.com

You know you're a good reporter when you get thrown out of the country

Nellie also traveled to Mexico for a time, and sent back stories about the changes unfolding there. Her stories were not always flattering to the government, and they eventually got her thrown out of the country.

There was nowhere Margaret wouldn't go for a photograph. She would snowshoe to logging camps, hang out of helicopters, and clamber up construction-site girders to capture an image she knew was right. If the action was at the front lines or across the globe, she made sure she was there, camera in hand. With amazing daring and talent, Margaret Bourke-White captured four decades on film, and helped shape the way we saw them.

Margaret gained early attention in New York City as the "little girl photographer" who balanced on a gargoyle outside her upper-floor studio in the Chrysler Building (then the tallest building in the world) in order to get a perfect shot.

She was among the first *Fortune* and *Life* magazine photographers, and her rendering of the Fort Peck Dam graced the cover of *Life*'s first issue. In 1930, Margaret was the first Western photographer allowed into the Soviet Union. She took pictures of industry and social conditions for *Fortune* and created a book about Russian industry called *Eyes on Russia*.

In the mid-1930s, Margaret shifted her focus to human subjects. She spent months traveling with writer Erskine Caldwell, who later became

her husband. Together they documented the lives of drought victims in America's Dust Bowl, impoverished sharecroppers in the South, and life in Czechoslovakia before the Nazi invasion. They published three books of their collaborative work, but eventually went their separate ways. Margaret continued to pursue her true passion on her own.

Margaret paid tribute to her mom by adding her maiden name, Bourke, to her own last name when she was twenty-two.

In 1945, Margaret marched across the Rhine River into Germany with General Patton's army and was among the first photographers at the Nazi death camps. Her pictures of the emaciated inmates and corpses in gas chambers were collected in the book, *Dear Fatherland, Rest Quietly.*

AT THE FRONT

When World War II broke out, Margaret headed for where the action was. She survived a torpedo attack on her way to North Africa, becoming the first woman photographer to see action in North Africa and Italy. She was the first accredited female war photographer and the first woman to fly a combat mission. Margaret documented the daily struggles of infantrymen and later covered the siege of Moscow.

After the war, Margaret photographed Mahatma Gandhi in India and fierce fighting in the Korean War. In the early 1950s, her career was curtailed when she was diagnosed with Parkinson's disease. Margaret devoted her time to writing and continued to take pictures when she could. She died in 1971 having produced some of the most important photographs of the twentieth century.

DOROTHEA LANGE

When Dorothea Lange graduated from high school in 1913, she was determined to become a photographer—despite the fact that she knew little about the work and had never used a camera. But Lange had spent much of her childhood observing people in her New Jersey hometown and wanted to document what she saw.

So Dorothea apprenticed with photographers, then bought her own camera, using a converted chicken coop as a darkroom. Eventually she made her way to San Francisco, where she became a successful society photographer.

In the early 1930s, Lange became overwhelmed by the daily misery she witnessed among victims of the Great Depression. She abandoned her lucrative career in order to devote her energy to documenting their plight. Dorothea traveled the country taking pictures of the rural poor. Her photographs increased public sympathy for the impoverished and contributed to the development of relief programs throughout the country.

Calamity Jane

was the **RIP**-roarin'est, **GUN**-totin'est, **HARD**-ridin'est gal to ever stampede the **WILD** West. Back when women were supposed to be home seeing to the young 'uns, **Calamity Jane** came along and showed 'em all how a real cowgirl took charge. She might have dressed like a man, but Calamity was all woman, and would shoot the hat off of any man who said otherwise.

In the mid-1800s when a woman's place was definitely in the home, Calamity Jane was out on the American frontier hunting, riding, and living a life of high adventure. In the down-and-dirty untamed West, Calamity had no time for acting like a lady—she swore, drank in saloons, and wore men's clothing. She was a savvy gambler and an ace with a rifle.

And since Calamity was never shy about retelling the stories of her adventures, there are plenty of accounts on the books. Of course, she was also known for stretching the truth for the sake of a good yarn, so not all of her reports can be taken at face value. But Calamity wasn't about to let a few nitpickers ruin a good story.

HOW MARTHA "CALAMITY JANE" CANNARY GOT HER NICKNAME

One Captain Egan and his troops were being beaten steadily by band of marauding Indians when Egan was wounded. Martha rode into the melee and, the way she tells it, "got there in time to catch him as he was falling [off his horse]." She hoisted the captain onto her saddle and rode out unscathed.

Martha saved Egan's life while the rest of the men perished. Upon recovering, the captain dubbed her "Calamity Jane, heroine of the plains," presumably because of the way she faced calamity head-on and always prevailed.

Her autobiography, *Calamity Jane, Written by Herself* has been disputed by a few spoil-sports, but the fact is that even half of Calamity's claimed adventures would have qualified her as a bonified legend.

Martha Jane Cannary was born in Missouri in 1848 and traveled across the Wild West with her family. By the time she was sixteen, her parents were dead and she was alone in the world. In writing about her early years, Martha says she "became an expert rider . . . able to ride the most vicious and stubborn of horses" over the roughest of terrain. By thirteen she was hunting along with the men—"In fact," she writes, "I was at all times along with the men when there was excitement or adventures to be had."

As a teenager, Martha roamed the mining districts working as a cook, a dance hall girl, and a muleskinner. By eighteen, she was performing dangerous missions for General Custer's forces in battles against the Indians. Never one for modesty, Calamity wrote, "I was considered the most reckless and daring rider and one of the best shots in the western country." She also was a scout in General Crook's army under Buffalo Bill Cody, who spoke admiringly of her unlimited nerve, telling how she'd travel in places where other frontiersmen were afraid to go.

During her time in the Black Hills, Calamity Jane befriended the legendary Wild Bill Hickock. Soon after they met, he was shot in a saloon and Calamity Jane swore to avenge his death. She found the rogue murderer Jack

On one occasion Calamity single-handedly rescued six men when Indians attacked their stagecoach.

McCall at the local butcher shop and held him up with a meat cleaver until reinforcements came. He was later tried, sentenced, and hung.

Calamity Jane next "retired" at the ripe old age of twenty-nine and took up ranching on the Yellowstone reserve. She also kept a wayside inn. But Calamity became restless soon enough and hit the trail, winding up in Texas where she met and married Clinton Burke. They had a baby girl, but their marriage didn't last long. Soon Calamity Jane was back on the road, traveling through the Northwest.

Rumors say she was fired for erratic behavior and alcoholism when she appeared at the Pan-American Exposition in New York in 1901. Possibly by this time her wild ways had caught up with her, for Calamity Jane retreated to the Black Hills town of Deadwood where she died in 1903.

Local people remembered her as a saint because of the way she helped nurse the sick during a smallpox epidemic, and stories of Calamity Jane's bravery and irreverence have continued to flourish long after her demise.

Belle Starr – The Bad Girl

Belle Starr committed the crimes, but was she a victim of the times . . . or was she actually as bad as her rap sheet implies?

Myra Belle Shirley earned renown as a thief and rustler in Texas and Oklahoma of the late 1800s. And she didn't balk at an occasional murder. Although the activities that made Belle famous too often found her on the wrong side of the law, she certainly challenged social preconceptions about women.

Before her life of crime, Belle was a guerrilla fighter in the Civil War but was unfortunate enough to end up on the losing side. (After the war, guerrillas were posted as outlaws, which forced them to become fugitives.)

Though many would like to blame Belle's life of shady dealings on a deficient upbringing or a slew of bad-egg boyfriends, others have made a case against the Union, politics, and fate.

Regardless of the cause of her transgressions, Belle Starr played the bandit queen role to the hilt—decking herself out in glamorous velvet and feathers, sometimes opting for the earthy buckskin-and-moccasin look, and changing outlaw boyfriends as often as most women change their hairstyles. (Granted, it's difficult to keep relationships going if your boyfriends keep getting killed.)

Maria *Callas* The Ultimate Diva

Maria Callas became the most celebrated opera star in history not because of her flawless voice, but because of the raw emotion she brought to her work. Maria knew she was born to be a diva, and simply made it so.

Maria burst onto the world's opera stage with a storybook entrance—she stepped into a sick soprano's part in *Tosca* when she was only eighteen, and brought down the house. Callas wowed critics and fans alike with the intense emotion and artistry of her performance.

Maria didn't just sing her roles, or even simply act them—she LIVED them with a kind of intensity that the opera world had been missing, and she became known for her incredibly exciting performances. Soon, her performances set the standard for almost every role she portrayed, and her imperfect voice seemed only to enhance the emotion of her singing. Her vitality brought new popularity to opera and new life to many older operas that had long been neglected.

By the time she was twenty-four, Callas was all the rage. She was performing an impressive fifty times a year to sold-out opera houses and by 1951, she'd established herself as prima donna at La Scala, Milan's leading opera house.

Some say Maria's undoing was falling in love with the wrong man. Around the time her voice began to fail, Callas met Aristotle Onassis, the billionaire tycoon. She left her husband and gave her life over to a whirlwind of parties, yachting excursions, and romantic ups and downs. This lifestyle was hardly conducive to resting her voice and Callas contracted a throat disease.

After setting a precedent of up to fifty performances a year, she performed fewer than thirty from 1960 to 1964, and from 1965 to 1973 she didn't perform at all. The press watched closely as her professional life as well as her personal life deteriorated.

At forty-five, the diva who had so recently had the world at her feet found herself with not much of a career and without the man she'd compromised it for. She had a breakdown, and though in the years that followed she made several comeback attempts, her voice never regained its luster. The critics were ruthless in reporting their disappointment.

All **Divas** are entitled to an occasional tantrum

. . . and Maria was no exception. Her temper could be wicked, and it was riled even more by the relentless media attention she received. In 1958, Callas actually refused to continue a performance in Rome after the first act—the Italian president was left waiting in the audience.

"Singing for me is not an act of pride, but an effort to elevate towards those heavens where everything is harmony."

Maria died in 1977 at age fifty-three, having spent her final years in Paris. Fittingly, her ashes were scattered in the Aegean Sea during a storm.

Early Burn-Out: The CURSE of the Superstar

Like so many of the greatest stars [think Janis Joplin or Billie Holiday], Maria was probably doomed by the intensity of her own talent and passion. Opera singers, like great athletes, must be careful to pace themselves in order to preserve their talent. But Maria refused to bend to these constraints and took on the most demanding roles with relentless determination. But as the rigors of her performance schedule and media scrutiny began to take their toll, Callas' voice began to show signs of strain. She began canceling performances and fell out of favor with many of the opera houses.

Did LOVE do her wrong?

Maria's relationship with Onassis deteriorated throughout the 1960s, and when he married Jacqueline Kennedy in 1968, Callas was devastated.

Maria Callas did deliver an occasional command performance during those years, but her greatest contribution came in the master classes she taught in the early 1970s at the Juilliard School in New York City. As a teacher, Callas imparted the wisdom of a diva to young singers. Her classes became legendary and later were immortalized in Terrance McNally's Broadway play, *Master Class.*

Cleopatra

QUEEN OF THE NILE

Cleopatra was the consummate femme fatale—brilliant, seductive, and dangerous—and probably the most famous female ruler in all of history.

Cleo had an insatiable craving for power, and her dream was to create a world empire with herself as the empress. Quick-witted and wildly determined, she came very close to achieving just that. But Cleopatra was more than just a pretty face with wily ways—she had the brains to back up her ambition. She is said to have been fluent in nine languages, an excellent mathematician, and the shrewdest of businesswomen.

Known as the "Queen of Kings," Cleopatra was just seventeen when she inherited her father's Macedonian empire in 51 B.C. Because women weren't allowed to rule in those days, she had to marry her fifteen-year-old brother, Ptolemy XIII. Cleopatra soon dropped his name from official documents and had her own portrait put on the local coins.

Cleopatra did what she felt was necessary to maintain power and benefit Alexandria; and thus came her reputation for determination and extravagant plots. When apprised of a secret meeting between her brother and Julius Caesar, ruler of the Roman Empire, Cleopatra snuck through enemy lines and charmed Caesar into siding with her (see "She Knew How to Work It"). Cleopatra's brother died fleeing Caesar's forces.

Cleo had to marry her next brother in line. But after the ceremony she set off with Caesar and they settled in a palace near Rome, despite their both being married.

SO SHE WASN'T A SAINT . . .

Eventually Caesar was assasinated by his disapproving countrymen and Cleopatra returned to Egypt. She promptly had her brother knocked off, took power with her and Caesar's four-year-old son as consort, and waited to see who would gain Roman rule.

When it seemed Marc Antony had the upper hand, Cleopatra plotted her next move. She secured Antony's heart, but again she had gambled on the losing team. Antony was defeated by Octavian and Cleo was left desperate for a plan. She had word sent to Antony that she was dead, hoping that the message would induce him to kill himself. Cleopatra figured that their "tragic love story" would win them undying renown. Meanwhile, she would attempt to make a place for herself in Octavian's empire. But—for once—her powers of seduction failed. Octavian was unmoved.

Since women weren't allowed to rule in Cleopatra's day, she wa forced to marry two of her brothers (in succession) to provide a male figurehead. This was a small formality to Cleo and, of course, did nothi to slow down her romar tic life. Besides, Cleopat wasn't much of a big si ter anyway—she went war against one brother and had another execute

Cleopatra is easily the most glamorous ruler in Egypt's history, and is often called the "Queen of the Nile," after the country's mightiest river.

Left: Theda Bara in the film *Cleopatra* (Fox, 1917)

AN ENDING FIT FOR AN EGYPTIAN QUEEN

Rather than live as a slave in Octavian's empire (which included cities she had once ruled), Cleopatra VII, at the age of thirty-nine, clutched an Egyptian cobra to her breast and allowed it to take a fatal bite. The asp, a symbol of Egyptian royalty, was believed to assure its victim immortality.

She knew how to work it

A man in Cleopatra's determined sights didn't stand a chance. Take the time she tried to head off her brother in Julius Caesar's chambers: Cleopatra had herself rolled in an Oriental carpet and smuggled through enemy lines. The carpet was presented to Caesar, and sure enough its contents charmed him senseless. Caesar helped defeat Cleo's brother and spent the rest of his life by her side.

After Caesar died, Cleo set her sights on Marc Antony. She dressed herself as Aphrodite, the goddess of love, and set sail. She arrived at his camp in a silver-oared boat with purple sails, her Erotes fanning her and Nereid handmaids steering. She knew Antony would find this display irresistible. And she was right—he abandoned his wife and ran away with Cleo to live in Alexandria.

23

COMIC BOOK QUEENS

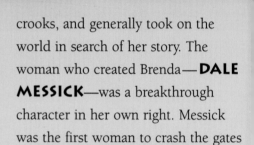

Blond Bombers and Girl Commandos–

The names of the female characters that stormed into the comic strips of the 1940s say it all. In a kind of pop culture explosion of feminism, these comic strips were suddenly filled with fierce new super-heroines who redefined the medium. *Who created these fantastic femme fatales?* **Women, of course.** Behind the greatest girl heros were great female minds—

the **Comic Book Queens** of the 1940s.

A lthough women had been drawing comic strips prior to the 1940s, their work had been limited to "light" or "cutesy" characters and storylines. The world of action-adventure was still the exclusive territory of men. This fact was reflected in the strips— action heros were always men, and although women were allowed to be

beautiful, they were never particularly active. Female characters, when they appeared, did so only to be rescued by the men.

Enter Brenda Starr. Strong, brash, and wildly independent— Brenda was a revelation in comic strip imagery. Billed as the "plucky" girl reporter, Brenda was clearly a woman in charge of her own destiny. She jumped out of planes, chased after

crooks, and generally took on the world in search of her story. The woman who created Brenda—**DALE MESSICK**—was a breakthrough character in her own right. Messick was the first woman to crash the gates of action comics, despite plenty of

resistance to her ideas. Her persistence paid off when Brenda Starr was a hit. The famous "girl reporter" inspired an enthusiastic female following, and eventually become one of the most beloved women comic strip characters of all time.

And then came Miss Fury.

Debuting in 1942, Miss Fury was a natural successor to Brenda Starr. She was exciting and strong, and had the added appeal of being a costumed superheroine. (Miss Fury was actually the alter ego of glamorous heiress Marla Drake, who would make her transformation by slipping into a panther-skin outfit.)

One publisher turned down Messick's comic strip proposal because he said "he had tried a woman cartoonist once . . . and wanted no more of them."

Once again, it had taken a woman to create such a compelling female character. **TARPÉ MILLS** was nearly as colorful as the characters she drew, and the media loved to point out the similarities between her and the fictional Marla Drake. After learning to draw at the Pratt Institute in New York, Mills had drawn for he-man action strips before finally selling the fabulous "Miss F" in 1941.

The public thrilled to the exploits of characters like Miss Fury and Brenda Starr, and the doors to great superheroines (and the women who

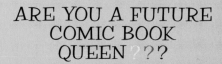

ARE YOU A FUTURE COMIC BOOK QUEEN???

CHECK OUT THESE SOURCES

♛ BOOKS BY TRINA ROBBINS
A Century of Women Cartoonists
The Great Women Superheroes
(Kitchen Sink Press)

♛ FRIENDS OF LULU
Web site: www.friends-lulu.org
4657 Cajon Way
San Diego, CA 92115

wanted to draw them) were officially wide open. In came fantastic comic strips like *Girl Commandos, Blond Bomber,* and *Toni Gayle, Girl Detective* —all drawn by women following in the footsteps of the first and most fabulous

Comic Book Queens.

Like many women comic strip artists, both Dale Messick and Tarpé Mills (born June Mills) changed their names to something more androgynous to disguise the fact that their strips were drawn by women.

Madame Curie

In 1891, Marie Curie walked into the boys club of the science world and basically tore the place apart.

Not that she really meant to—Marie didn't *want* to cause trouble, but she was so brilliant that she couldn't help but smash through cozy stereotypes with every new breakthrough discovery. Since most fields of science were closed to women at the turn of the century, Marie started by discovering her own—radiology. When they wouldn't let her into the prestigious Academy of Science, she won a Nobel Prize in physics to press the point. And after there was some talk about the first one being a fluke, she won another Nobel (in chemistry) just to set the record straight.

Marie was brainy from the start, winning top honors in all of her studies. After she lost both her mother and sister to disease, she became committed to the cause of science as a means of major medical advancement. But after graduation, her family's lack of money and her status as a woman prevented her from following her career, and she took a position as a tutor and governess. She made a deal to send her sister to medical school, in return for the same favor someday.

She finally journeyed to Paris in 1891, where she met and married Pierre Curie. She hit on the natural occurrence of radioactivity (a term which she coined) and, along with Pierre and Henri Becquel, won a Nobel Prize for physics in 1903—the first woman to do so. Pierre was killed in a traffic accident in 1906—a devastating event for Marie, but one that renewed her determination to continue their work. She was appointed to a professorship at the Sorbonne—another first for a woman—and went on to win another Nobel in chemistry when she managed to isolate radium in its pure form.

26

Did She Touch That Stuff?

Of course. That's what was so courageous about Marie's work. Even though she and her husband Pierre were partially aware of the damaging effects of radiation, they continued to handle uranium ore with their bare hands. They routinely developed blisters on their hands, and their science journals are still radioactive today. In older age, Marie was nearly blind and unable to use her fingers because of her work—she died of leukemia that was likely the result of her early exposure to radiation.

Marie Goes to WAR

Marie wasn't much on ivory towers. In World War I, she knew that her X-ray treatment was a great way to pinpoint bullets and shrapnel in wounded soldiers, and converted 150 cars into "X-ray mobiles." In gratitude for her heroic efforts, in 1921 she was presented with a gram of radium in a ceremony by the American Association of University Women.

So WHAT Did She Discover?

So now imagine that weird periodic table your chemistry teacher was always breathlessly waving a stick at. Remember how smart (and just a little scary) you thought that girl in class was who memorized it? Well, Marie was the kind of woman who *added* to it.

Whoa. She's responsible for exactly two boxes. Radium (with hubby Pierre) and Pollonium.

But, believe it or not, Marie wasn't all that interested in being another question for you to sweat on your chemistry test. Here's what she wanted from her work and exactly what she got:

More Curie Trivia . . .

★ Marie's daughter Irene followed her into science, and, with her husband, also won a Nobel Prize for the discovery of artificial radioactivity. She died of leukemia only a year after her mother—also likely brought on by her work with radiation.

★ Marie's ashes were enshrined at the Pantheon in Paris—the first woman to be given this honor.

★ Marie and Pierre refused to patent their process for isolating radium—wanting all scientists to have access to its applications, and throwing away the financial security it would have brought them.

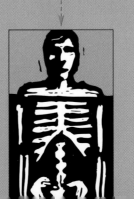

◉ Cancer Treatment

◉ X-Rays

◉ Dating Technique

◉ Molecular Biology

◉ Nuclear Physics

The Babe

Babe Didrikson Zaharias was the closest thing to a *superwoman* that real life has ever seen. She blew into the world of sports like a one-woman force of nature, and simply, awesomely, established herself as the best all-round athlete of the century— quite possibly of all time. Melodramatic?

Let's review the record:

AFTER EARNING HER NICKNAME for routinely whacking the ball out of the park in neighborhood softball games, Babe moves on to basketball, where she quickly leads her team to the national championship. She is named the *Associated Press (AP)* Female Athlete of the Year, for the first of **what would be six times.** In her spare time, she fits in a little barnstorming with the legendary women's baseball team, the *House of David.*

1920s

AT THE OLYMPIC TRIALS IN CHICAGO, Babe confuses officials when she shows up alone, until they realize that **she is an entire team.** She competes in eight events, breaking **four** world records. She is hurriedly sent to the Olympics later that year, where she is disappointed to learn that she can compete in only **three** events. So she only wins **three** events, and sets **three** world records.(But only snags two gold medals—a stingy judge keeps the high jump gold medal from her on a technicality.)

1932

BABE DECIDES TO GIVE GOLF A TRY, and things being how they are, wins the women's golf championship the next year. She decides to stick with this sport, and wins forty tournaments in four years. **Including seventeen in a row.** She helps to found the LPGA, and wins the U.S. Women's Open in 1948, 1950, and 1954. In 1950, the *AP,* having run out of awards to give her, simply names her Best Female Athlete of the Half Century and lets it go at that.

1935

Any questions?

Babe Takes on the Brits

The Babe blew the Brits away with a combination of awesome physicality and personal style the likes of which they had never seen. Babe was brash, brazen, and braggartly in a performance that sprang straight from her Texas roots. The British crowds were at first alarmed, then enthusiastic, and finally *wild* about the Babe.

ONE OF BABE'S MOST legendary triumphs came at the British Women's Amateur Golf Championship in 1947. She was personally intent on winning the tournament, considering it critical that she prove herself a champion on both sides of the Atlantic. The press expected her to tone down her style for the English, who were more reserved, more civilized about their sports. **The press, of course, was wrong.**

During one of her first days, Babe complained about the quiet crowds, and began showboating shamelessly, clowning and talking to the onlookers. The Brits were startled, and some wondered if Babe had gone too far. Of course, her show was just beginning, and Babe began to pull out her trick shots. She began by putting a match behind her tee-off, so that her shot exploded on impact. Later, she hit two balls out of a sandtrap at once—one landed in her pocket and the other in the hole. The Brits' reserve was broken, and they began cheering wildly. That's when Babe, on the eighteenth hole, turned around, and knocked in the final shot of the day—between her legs. The gallery exploded in a near riot of adoration and disbelief.

The Babe had won the hearts of the British exactly as she had planned—by sheer force of talent and bravado. Her tournament finale was the perfect ending gesture. After her final, winning shot, Babe touched up her lipstick for the cameras, and suddenly hurdled a wall for photographers, recalling her track and field days. They haven't forgotten her since.

That's when Babe, on the eighteenth hole, turned around and knocked in the final shot of the day between her legs.

The Fastest Women on Earth — More Olympic Superstars

- **Wilma Rudolph** rebounded from a childhood marked by polio and leg braces to become the first woman to earn three gold medals in the Olympics; winning the 100, 200, and 4 x 100 relay.

- In 1988, **Florence Griffith-Joyner "Flo-Jo"** repeated this exact medal-winning performance. Her sister-in-law, **Jackie Joyner-Kersee** won the gold medal in the heptathlon (which includes seven events) in both 1988 and 1992.

29

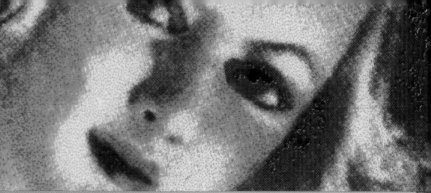

Nancy Drew

Girl, Nancy had it all

THINK ABOUT IT. She could ride a horse, play golf, downhill ski, scuba dive, and pilot a sailboat to safety in a hurricane. Nancy always knew where the secret passageway was. She was an expert on any subject that came up, including car repair, jewel appraisal, and ancient map deciphering. She understood the mystery behind any given hidden diary or shady glen, and she wasn't afraid of the castle on the hill.

Nancy knew who sent the warning to GET OFF THE CASE, and that the haunted mansion wasn't. Her car was a convertible, her complexion was clear, and her relationships trouble-free. Nancy had a boyfriend, a father, and flat shoes when it was convenient, and *never any time else.*

Nancy was eighteen. Forever. Nancy was smart, strong, competent, brave, dependable, kind, poised, resourceful, and wildly, gloriously ordinary. Nancy was every girl's secret refuge of rightness, and every girl's ticket to adventure without fear.

That was true blue Nancy Drew.

Who could compete with Nancy?

One of the qualities that makes us love Bess and George is that they don't even try. They're the most loyal of sidekicks, never seeming to resent their secondary status next to Nancy's starring role. Together, they provide the perfect contrast to Nancy's flawlessly executed competence.

They're also a perfect contrast to each other—George, of course, is the tomboy, while Bess plays the part of the fluttering coquette. George is tough and brave, but has none of Nancy's composure under pressure. Flirty Bess is entertaining and enthusiastic but flighty too often when it counts.

Nancy, ever-tolerant, serenely accepts both the good and the bad in her two best friends—and always comes off as the heroine. And that's what a good sidekick is all about.

THE NANCY DREW FILES™

PUBLISHED BY POCKET BOOKS/AN ARCHWAY PAPERBACK

121
NATURAL ENEMIES
CAROLYN KEENE

Nancy Drew Case #121, 1997

Who was Carolyn Keene?

Sure, we all know the name that appears on all of the Nancy Drew covers. But who was she, really? A few different people, it turns out, including two strong women who passed on much of their own energy to our favorite girl detective.

Nancy was first conceived of by Edward Stratemeyer in the late 1920s, following his success with the Hardy Boys series. He wrote the first three books, and the job passed on to a number of writers after his death. His daughter, **Harriet Adams,** is probably most responsible for carrying on Nancy's flame. Harriet was somewhat of a bold character herself, running her father's company (along with her sister) and making sure that Nancy Drew's strong image stayed true to her father's vision. And you can't mention Nancy Drew without giving a nod to **Mildred Wirt Benson**—one of the most prolific writers of Nancy's stories. She was nearly as adventurous as her famous subject—Benson was the first woman to receive a master's degree from the University of Iowa School of Journalism in 1927. She was a licensed pilot and often flew herself to her far-reaching destinations. She was keenly interested in archaelogy, which led to a wide and exotic travel record.

So to all the creators behind Carolyn Keene: we say, thanks for the adventure, the stories, and the inspiration —thanks for our fabulous Nancy Drew.

There have been other ghostwriters behind the famous Carolyn Keene pseudonym, all of whom can be credited with keeping Nancy bold and independent. Today we take those qualities for granted, but when Edward Stratemeyer first introduced them, they were considered breakthrough qualities in a female character. Girls loved it—the Nancy Drew series was a smash hit despite the hardships of the Great Depression. Since that introduction, Nancy Drew stories have sold more than **sixty million copies** worldwide for nearly seventy years, making Nancy Drew one of the most influential female characters of all time.

Amelia Earhart

THE MOST GLAMOROUS FLY-GIRL

For a brief time in history, Amelia Earhart represented everything that was exciting about the American dream. Adventure, optimism, and the glamour of a movie star—the lady pilot with the shy smile and the aviator scarf had it all. To a country in the throes of the Great Depression, every record she set spoke of a future that would be brighter someday, even prosperous. As for Amelia, her dreams had little to do with celebrity or parades, and everything to do with the call of the unknown.

Because what Amelia loved, more than anything else, was to fly.

Amelia took Eleanor Roosevelt up in her plane, after which the First Lady declared her intention to learn to fly. But Eleanor was already notorious for her fast driving, and President Roosevelt quickly said that he had enough to worry about as it was.

AMELIA was born in Atchison, Kansas, on July 24, 1897. She was ten years old when she saw her first plane at the Iowa State Fair and she was not impressed. "It was a thing of rusty wire and wood and not at all interesting," she later said.

When Amelia was twenty-three though, she went to an air show in California with her dad and was suddenly struck with flying fever. She took her first flying lesson, and a few months later had scraped together the money to buy a Kinner Airster Aircraft.

Amelia worked lots of odd jobs (including hauling gravel) so that she'd have enough cash to keep flying. After gaining fame for crossing the Atlantic as a passenger in 1928, Amelia decided to fly the same trip solo four years later. She was the first woman to do so, and even set a new record for speed (2,026 miles in fourteen hours). Inflight, she used smelling salts to stay awake, and brought only a thermos of soup and a can of tomato juice for food.

But she was unprepared for the public's reaction. Amelia returned to a ticker-tape parade in New York City, and President Herbert Hoover personally awarded her a medal for her contribution to aviation. She accepted several of her awards on behalf of "all women."

The U.S. Coast Guard cutter *Itasca* picked up Amelia's last transmission:

"KHAQQ calling Itasca. We must be on you but cannot see you . . . gas is running low . . ."

AMELIA MARY EARHART jumped into cockpits during a time when air travel was very new; people simply did not casually step onto planes to go visit their grandmothers—or for any other reason.

Although Amelia became one of the most famous women in the world during her lifetime, the private Amelia disliked her fame intensely. She was definitely not getting airborne to show off. "My ambition is to have this wonderful gift produce practical results for the future of commercial flying and for the women who may want to fly tomorrow's planes," she said.

THE DISAPPEARANCE: A FEW THEORIES

- Amelia lived for years on an island in the South Pacific with a fisherman.
- The trip was actually a spy mission Amelia was sent on by President Roosevelt and she was captured.
- Amelia dove her plane into the Pacific on purpose.
- Amelia was captured by the Japanese and forced to broadcast to American GIs as "Tokyo Rose" during World War II.
- Amelia's still alive. There have been many unconfirmed sightings . . . she would be 100 years old if she were alive today.

WHAT'S YOUR THEORY?

THE FINAL FLIGHT

Amelia's plan was to be the first pilot—of either sex—to fly around the world at the equator (the longest way possible). After a false start that ended in a crash on takeoff, her plane was repaired, and Amelia and her navigator Fred Noonan took off from Miami, Florida on June 1, 1937.

Flying eastward, they stopped for fuel, repairs, and rest in exotic cities along the way. They completed 22,000 miles of the 29,000 mile trip before they vanished on July 2, 1937.

Amelia had just cabled her last article to the *Herald Tribune* from New Guinea, and photos showed her looking tired and sick.

The country was stunned. For more than two weeks, a full-scale search ensued and President Roosevelt authorized the use of U.S. military planes and ships in the effort.

Gradually, as time passed, the world began to accept the loss of their favorite aviator. Although a number of theories about her disappearance have surfaced, the most probable explanation is that she and her copilot crashed into the ocean, dying on impact or drowning soon after.

It was a tragic end to such an exciting life, but Amelia left behind a permanent legacy—a generation of women with a new sense of their own potential. She would have liked knowing that her life inspired hope instead of fear, and, ironically, expressed exactly that sentiment in a final letter to her husband:

"Women must try to do things as men have tried. When they fail their failure must be but a challenge to others."

EVITA

She's the very familiar, beautiful woman in elaborate 1940s hairdos, hats and jewelry; idolized by millions and considered a saint by some. There are books, plays, and songs about her. Madonna played her in a movie. So powerful is the glamorous image of her that it is sometimes forgotten that Evita Perón was about more than just being fabulous.

Evita, born Eva Maria Ibarguraen, started out life in a small, poor Argentina town, one of five children of an impoverished single mother. Maybe her hard childhood instilled in her the compassion for the poor which was always at the heart of her political message. Certainly it made the perfect beginning for the story of Evita the legend.

In 1935, when Evita was only fifteen, she left home for Buenos Aires, escaping her small town with a tango singer who was performing there briefly. It didn't matter that she was not particularly talented; her dogged pursuit of acting roles, together with her skill at making friends with the right people, made her a success, particularly in radio. On the radio she created and perfected a public persona, even starring in a series, "The Heroines of History." Evita would later use radio to advance her political career and to rally the masses behind the ideals of Perónism, the political ideology of her husband, Juan Perón.

An avid feminist, Evita formed the Association for Women's Suffrage, and was ultimately responsible for Argentine women getting the vote in 1947. She wrote: *"We are absent from government. We are absent from parliaments . . . And yet we have always been present in the time of suffering, and in all humanity's bitter hours."*

Colonel Juan Perón was vice president, minister of war and secretary of labor when Evita met him. He was forty-eight, she twenty-four. They quickly became an item. Evita and Perón were essential to each other's careers. She stumped for him on the radio, speaking as "the voice of a woman of the people," while he appointed her to a variety of positions, beginning with head of the Radio Association of Argentina.

When Juan Perón was elected president in 1946, it was almost certainly due to Evita's brilliant behind-the-scenes campaigning. It was Evita who orchestrated the "impromptu" speeches to streets full of cheering crowds—one of Perón's hallmarks that made him a champion of the people.

Evita married Perón five days before his election. As First Lady she was a maverick and a contradiction. She continued to dress as a glamorous actress while she tirelessly worked on behalf of Argentina's poorest citizens— the *descamisados,* or "shirtless ones." Evita rattled the establishment by appearing alongside her husband at presidential speeches, performing official and unofficial government work on her own, and wearing smashing, shoulder-baring evening gowns to formal state functions.

Tragically, Evita was struck down by cancer when she was only thirty-three. Toward the end of her life, when her body was ravaged by disease, she continued to work obsessively. Her doctor quit in exasperation in 1950, after she rebuked him for telling her not to work so hard.

Though she became increasingly ill, Evita worked exhausting days as First Lady. She sometimes received

hundreds of visitors in a single day and personally answered tens of thousands of letters. A compassionate woman, a public relations genius, or both, Evita kept a pile of cash on her desk, which she would hand out to visitors. Those who came included Argentina's most needy. These she received warmly, sometimes embracing and kissing them.

By the time Evita died in 1952, she was a legend. Millions mourned her passing. Her husband, beginning his second term as president, determined that every Argentine who wanted to should be allowed to view her body. That goal proved impossible as lines stretched thirty blocks in every direction for days.

So powerful was the persona Evita had created that even after her death, divided factions battled over her body. She was moved several times. An enormous crypt was constructed for her burial and then dynamited before she ever got there. In a bizarre twist, her body disappeared completely for almost fifteen years, eventually turning up in Italy under a false name. In 1976, Evita was finally returned to Argentina and properly buried.

EVITA WORSHIP

At one of Evita's speeches, the crowd was so enthusiastic that at least seven people were crushed to death. . . . When Evita made an official visit to Spain, three million people greeted her. In Brazil on the same trip, she was dubbed "La Presidenta.". . . So dense and wild were the crowds gathered in the streets of Buenos Aires to mourn Evita's passing that 120,000 people were injured in a single day.

Janet Flanner

Has there ever been anything cooler than the Left Bank of Paris during the 1920s?

On most days, Janet Flanner could be found at Les Deux Magots Café on the Left Bank of the Seine River talking politics and culture with legendary American writers like Ernest Hemingway, F. Scott Fitzgerald, and Gertrude Stein. She was a central figure in Paris' café society between the world wars and became famous by writing about her experiences.

At the time, many creative people had left America in pursuit of political, social, and artistic freedom. They found Paris alluring and full of charm. The folks back home saw these expatriates as an intelligent and glamorous lot and followed their café gatherings with interest, curious about their opinions on everything from politics to whether life was better in Europe. Janet's perceptions about such matters were held in high regard, and early on she was asked to write a column for the *New Yorker* magazine documenting life in Paris.

Among the many subjects covered in Janet's *(Genêt's)* *Letter from Paris* was the execution by firing squad of the infamous Mata Hari (see "Lady Spies"). Janet reported her last words, and even commented on the outfit she wore.

Janet became famous for her "Letter from Paris" which appeared every other week under the pen name Genêt. She wrote pointedly, but with an ease and familiarity that gave readers a feeling of being privy to a clever conversation—the nature of which might occur at the cafés. She covered such momentous events as Hitler's rise to power and the Nuremberg trials, along with cultural topics that ranged from Parisian fashion to Josephine Baker's European debut (see Josephine's separate profile). Janet's unique style and the unconventional connections she made between diverse topics distinguished her writing and helped to make her one of the most influential writers on the Left Bank—and perhaps in the world. Her famous correspondence with America lasted for fifty years.

THE ART WORLD AND THE GIRL GENIUSES BEHIND THE SCENES

Cubism, modernism, new narrative—sometime around the 1920s the art and literary world exploded with all kinds of new innovations that had everybody talking. But to hear most people tell it, the only people fueling this revolution were men. *Wrong again, of course.* The truth is that names like Picasso, Hemingway, and James Joyce might not be famous today were it not for the genius of a few women who were ahead of their times.

As the owner of the world's most famous bookstore, **Sylvia Beach** was one of the most important influences on the literary set during the 1920s and 1930s. Like many other American women, Sylvia was drawn to Paris' cultural freedom, and when she opened the famous Shakespeare & Company bookstore, it was the realization of a dream. Along with her constant companion Adrienne Monnier, she turned the bookstore into a major European literary center. Sylvia was most famous for supporting the works of Irish author James Joyce when no one else would touch them—and in particular *Ulysses*. Today, *Ulysses* is recognized as one of the greatest novels of the twentieth century, but at the time it was condemned by critics and the public alike, who labeled it as "obscene." Sylvia alone recognized its importance, and published the novel despite the threat of being shut down and arrested.

When Sylvia Beach sold *Ulysses* in her bookstore, it was so dangerous that she often concealed it with a false cover.

A Fine Thank-You
Although Sylvia was almost single-handedly responsible for Joyce's introduction to the public, he abandoned her for another publisher when he was finally a commercial success.

Sylvia Beach

Althea Gibson

In 1936, the world watched Jesse Owens stand up to Hitler at the Berlin Olympics, and a decade later witnessed Jackie Robinson stepping across the color line of baseball. All the while, Althea Gibson was quietly building her skills at another game whose color barrier she would destroy. Against all odds, Althea would become the next great American hero, and, for a time, the greatest tennis player in the world.

Despite the racial breakthroughs of earlier decades, segregation still ruled the sports world of the 1950s, and nowhere more so than in the "genteel" game of tennis. The game had opened up to women, at least, and boasted new great stars like Hellen Wills and Alice Marble. While these new darlings of the tennis world were exciting to watch, they were also, as a group, very white. A "negro" player was allowed to play in the all-black ATA (American Tennis Association), which was a competitive and well-respected league, but provided a lower level of play than the tournaments like Forest Hills and Wimbledon. It's difficult to imagine today, but this system of segregated play operated smoothly for a time, without much pressure to change.

UNTIL ALTHEA. Now *she* was a problem. This player from the ATA with a relentless net game and a sizzling serve was clearly material for the big leagues. It was becoming obvious to fans and organizers alike that she was one of the best players of the game, regardless of race. To prove it, she won the singles championship for ten years at the ATA level. IN A ROW.

Althea was ready to move up. Her undeniable star potential was becoming an embarassment to the organizers of all-white tournaments—why wasn't she being invited to Forest Hills and Wimbledon? They were running out of excuses.

It took Alice Marble—one of the game's finest players—to finally speak out on Althea's behalf. She nailed the tennis establishment with the oft-quoted remark that Gibson was "not being judged by the yardstick of ability but by the fact that her pigmentation is somewhat different." This pressure proved to be the final straw, and in 1950 Althea was invited to Forest Hills, and the next year to Wimbledon.

Before the Color Break: The Stories We'll Never Know

Before Althea came **Ora Washington,** who played during the 1920s and 1930s. Like Althea, she dominated the American Tennis Association, winning twelve successive championships. When she challenged white tennis star Helen Wills to a game, Wills refused, and Washington was never allowed to play in the big leagues. Would she have been a world champion? We'll never know.

Althea's breakthrough to the major leagues of tennis was just as talked about as Jackie Robinson's had been in baseball. When she played at Forest Hills and Wimbledon, she was the first black person—of either sex—to ever do so. If the attention made her nervous, she never showed it: she played like a champion and worked to adjust her game to the new level of play.

Suddenly, in 1957, Althea's game exploded. That year, she took the singles titles at both Wimbledon and Forest Hills, and in 1958 won at Wimbledon again. These victories were a stunning personal success for the player who had begun the game on the rough streets of Harlem. But their importance from a social perspective cannot be overstated—Althea Gibson had single-handedly smashed the color barriers of tennis by being, for two glorious years, the best player in the world.

After all—how do you claim the game for an all-white audience when the best player in the

"Be polite to everybody and . . . beat the liver and lights out of the ball."

world is black? *You don't.* In tribute to her accomplishments, the *Associated Press* voted her the Woman Athlete of the Year in both 1957 and 1958. And *who knows* how far Althea Gibson might have gone if she'd been able to start in the big leagues as a teenager, as so many professional players do today? Remember—she wasn't allowed to play in the top pro circuit until she was twenty-three—years later than many players today.

Although 1958 would be the last year that she would be the top player, Althea went on to many other careers and interests. She played professional golf, wrote a book (*I Always Wanted to Be Somebody*), and helped other kids realize their own tennis dreams by organizing programs in inner-city neighborhoods.

But most of all, Althea Gibson will be remembered for the grace that she showed in the face of an ugly system, the year she changed the game of tennis forever.

Cool **Goddesses** *Before there were movie stars there were gods and goddesses.*

Star power, drama, sex appeal—they had it all, only with a different twist of mythic celebrity. Remember, this was way back in the B.C.-days of ancient history, when a fun night out meant swapping myths around the collonade. This dry set of circumstances put a lot of entertainment pressure on the myth-makers, to say the least, which might explain why some of the myths put today's tabloids to shame. So forget the celebrity magazines and the gossip shows—if you want a dose of real drama, take a look at some of the coolest goddesses on the books.

40

Isis

If there had been a popularity contest for Egyptian goddesses, **Isis** would have topped the list for three thousand years, beginning in about 3000 B.C. The goddess-happy Egyptians just couldn't get enough of her, it seems, and came to think of her as the supreme mother of the universe. To show their appreciation, they built one temple after another in her honor, and told more spectacular stories about her powers with every century.

Isis' popularity was rooted in a number of divine traits, but what really made her a superstar were her mythical powers of transformation, including the power to give life. Many of her exploits—like that with her husband Osiris (see sidebar)—are thought of as metaphors for the cycle of life and death.

Best Isis Story

When Isis' husband Osiris was killed and cut into pieces by another jealous god, Isis traveled the Nile gathering them up. When she had found them all, she put him back together again and revived him briefly with the power of her love. This must have been an exciting reunion: Isis and Osiris managed to conceive a child (Horus) during his brief comeback, who grew up to avenge the murder of his father.

Diana—THE HUNTRESS

Diana was another goddess with a fun gig—she was in charge of helping mortals with their hunting, and thus is usually depicted running around in the woods with her animal friends. Diana was beautiful, strong, and athletic, and so she had plenty of admirers, but none who could convince her to settle down. The stories starring Diana usually end with her refusal to give up her free ways in the forest (see sidebar). She was also linked with the cycles of the moon, and all of its associations with the rhythms of nature and female fertility.

Best Diana Story

In this story, one of Diana's less-gentlemanly admirers disguises himself in a deer skin and tries to spy on her while she bathes in the woods. Diana sees him and is not amused. She commands her dogs to attack, and the pitiful peeping tom is torn limb from limb. Although some would call this a good lesson about spying on hotheaded goddesses, most experts consider it a more symbolic tale about the rituals of the hunt.

Athena

As goddesses go, **Athena** had it all—as the goddess of wisdom *and* war she was considered brilliant, but not above using a little force when the situation called for it. According to Greek mythology, she was the favorite daughter of Zeus—the head honcho of Greek gods—which was probably why she got all of the fun goddess duties. The Greeks also thought of her as a muse of innovation, and gave her credit for some of their best ideas like the field plow and great architecture.

Best Athena Story

Legend has it that when the founders of Athens were deciding which deity's name should bless their new town, Zeus proposed a contest: the god or goddess who gave the city the best present would get the honor. Athena won hands down with her gift of the olive tree, which gave the Greeks shade from the sun, oil for their lamps, and, well, olives. Today, the legend of Athena's gift lives on in the symbolic stature of the olive wreath, which stands for peace and prosperity everywhere.

Oya

Think of **Oya** as the goddess of smart women everywhere. In Nigeria, when women are searching for just the right words to ease a tense situation, they ask Oya for help. And as with any woman secure in her own strength, Oya is mild-tempered during times of peace, but fierce when her anger is stirred. It is with these emotions that she is thought to rule the mighty Niger River. Legend has it that when Oya is content, she sends the river waters running smoothly, but when she is unhappy, she dries it up in a flash. And when she's really unhappy, she's apt to unleash a thunderstorm or two just to underline her point.

Best Oya Story

According to the myth of Oya, she was originally an antelope, but could take human form by stepping out of her antelope skin like a coat. When her future husband Shango spotted her in womanly form, he was hopelessly smitten, and convinced her to marry him. But he was so afraid that she would run away that he hid her antelope skin. Oya was sad to have lost her animal skin, and when she found that it was her husband's doing she was upset, to say the least. Shango managed to win her back with her favorite foods and sweet talk. They lived happily ever after, ruling their land and smiting their enemies together.

Jane Goodall

Braving the African wilds, challenging long-held assumptio◗ redefining the world of anthropology— Jane Goodall brought glamour back to the realm of research, and blew away every assumption about her field along the way.

It Takes Patience to Win Over a Chimp

It was six months before Goodall could get within five hundred yards of a chimp. *"For three hours I watched the chimps feeding. I was not only weary, but soaking wet from crawling through dense undergrowth."*

42

When Jane Goodall was about eight years old, the Dr. Doolittle story inspired her dream of living in Africa and writing about wild animals. Many years later, she saved her waitressing tips, left London, and sailed to Africa on the *Kenya Castle*. Jane did this despite the fact that while she was waiting tables, most people told her she was crazy. Why would someone want to work in Africa? Luckily, her mom believed in her, and said, *"If you work hard enough, take advantage of every opportunity, and never give up, you will find a way."* Today, Jane still lives by her mom's words.

How do you find work in Africa?

Once on African soil, Jane was faced with the prospect of find ing work in a foreign and intir dating culture. She dug in her heels and in 1957, she was hire by the world-famous anthropo gist and archaeologist Dr. Loui Leakey. *"He told me I was some◗ he had been seeking for ten years a girl to whom animals were mo◗ important than makeup, boyfrier and parties,"* Goodall offers. Leakey also liked that she was patient, an independent thinke and lived simply. These traits a came in handy during the six years she spent studying the chimps at the Gombe Stream chimpanzee reserve, where she lived in a tent with her mother Every day, they braved the thre of malaria, cobras, insects, and thieving baboons. Jane usually ate only once a day—in the evening. She would often leave the tent around dawn with not ing but a kettle of coffee to kee her going all day.

WANT TO KNOW MORE?

Call the Jane Goodall Institute 1-800-592-JANE and ask about the "Roots and Shoots" program

ane's Big reakthrough

e afternoon, while studying impanzees on the shores of ke Tanganyika in Africa, Jane w David Graybeard, one of her vorite chimps, using a grass m to poke a termite mound dig out the insects for his nch. She also saw chimps ipping down twigs to make ols. Who cares, right? Keep in nd that at this time, scientists nerally felt that what separated mans from chimps was that made and used tools. imps did not. Jane, a woman her twenties, with no college gree at the time (she couldn't ord it), had just *shredded* at theory.

Hey—Let's name the chimps.

Jane also revolutionized her field by considering the chimps to be individuals. In a world full of scientists who, she says, "chopped animals up to see how they worked," Jane was making breakthrough discoveries far from any laboratory simply by patiently observing the chimps in their natural habitat. She proved that chimpanzees are as individual in personality as humans, and that they have human-like relationships—she even dared to give them names.

DIAN FOSSEY, *Another African Trailblazer*

f it weren't for American anthropologist Dian Fossey, there might be no mountain gorillas alive today. Like Jane Goodall, she traveled to Africa, and revolutionized her field of study— gorillas. Dian studied her subjects in the mountains of Rwanda, one of the last places where the endangered mountain gorilla, living high in the mists of the Virunga volcanoes, still survived. Her work became dangerous when she began battling the poachers who were hunting and killing the gorillas. She organized teams of Rwandan anti-poaching rangers to cut traps, monitor gorilla health, and release trapped animals from snares. But Dian made many enemies during her crusade, and in 1985 she was murdered at her campsite. The killer was never found. Dian literally fought to the death for the cause she believed in.

"We have a choice to use the gift of our life to make the world a better place—or not to bother." —J. G.

NO WORK FOR SISSIES

Jane also took her share of hard knocks from the chimps. One surly male attacked her three times—very scary since she was on steep terrain. "He's really mean to me, and we don't know why," Goodall recorded. The last time he attacked her, Goodall hit her head on a rock and began bleeding. "Luckily small bushes stopped me from dropping to my death," Goodall said. The other chimps smelled her blood, seemed confused, and starting making "hoo-hooing" sounds. "There was nothing else for me to do but brush myself off and get back to the research center," she said. **Just another day at the office.**

Martha **Graham**

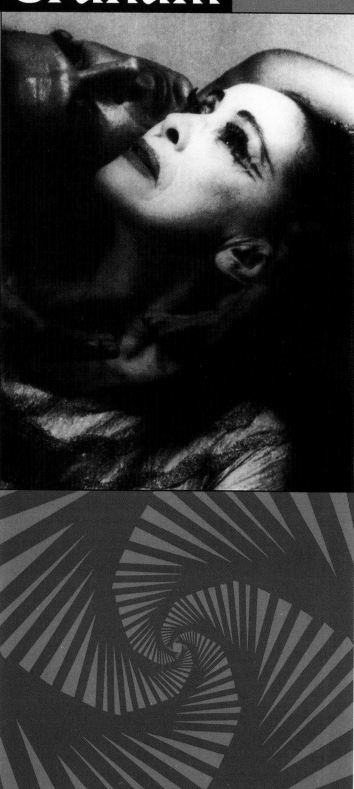

"Modern dance isn't anything except one thing in my mind: the freedom of women in America . . . It comes in as a moment of emancipation, the moment when an emergence took place from behind the bustle."

44

Before Martha hit the scene, classica ballet had been the standard in dance performance. Story lines were straightforward, movements graceful, and costumes decorative. Martha ripped into this pretty picture with a passion. She broke all the rules by creating dances with jagged, angular lines, distorted movements, and strong sexual tension. The critics were terrified—they called her dances "cold" and "unfeminine" and at one of her first stagings in Paris, the audience actually booed. But Martha held her ground, arguing,

"It's not my job to look beautiful. It's my job to look interesting."

To Martha, dance was a way to explore the spiritual and emotional essence of humanity and to communicate universal experiences. She used body movement to make the audience feel something instead o simply telling a story.

Headstrong from the start, Martha had decided at age seventeen that she would become a dancer after seeing a performance by Ruth St. Denis (see opposite page). "That night my fate was sealed," she said. Living by the sea in California also inspired Martha: she developed an appreciation for natural beauty and the rhythm of the ocean which was reflected in her work. Martha enrolled in dance school and eventu ally moved to New York, where she danced taught, and soon opened her own studio.

Untamed, stormy, rebellious—THINK OF MARTHA GRAHAM AS THE ULTIMATE WILD GIRL OF DANCE. WITH AN ABANDON THAT BLEW APART THE "FEMININE" DANCE WORLD OF TUTUS AND SWEETNESS, MARTHA CREATED HER OWN DANCES THAT WERE AS UNRULY AS THEY WERE BEAUTIFUL. CRITICS AND AUDIENCES WERE SHOCKED, BUT ULTIMATELY CAPTIVATED BY HER BRAVE NEW FORM. BY FORGING HER OWN ROAD, MARTHA GRAHAM CREATED MORE THAN A NEW STYLE OF DANCE—*she created a revolution.*

In 1936, Martha was invited to dance at the Olympic games in Germany. She refused, saying later, "It never entered my mind to say yes. How could I dance in Nazi Germany?"

The Amazons on Stage

For more than ten years, Martha's dance company featured only women, and her attitude toward femininity was an essential part of her rule-breaking style. She created strong, often dangerous female characters on stage, and told the stories of great women in history, including the poet Emily Dickinson and Joan of Arc.

She told her female dancers to forget their "little white wigs" and their "little toe shoes" and to embrace their power rather than hide it.

Eventually her themes began to call for men as well, and in 1939 she took on Merce Cunningham and Erick Hawkins. Erick danced as her partner and was also her husband for a short time.

But Don't Confuse WILD with UNDISCIPLINED

Martha was a fervent believer in the power of practice, maintaining that true creativity could not come until the basics of the craft had been mastered.

Her works demanded the most strenuous body-training method in the field of modern dance, and her methods of training are still practiced today.

As Young as You Feel

At the ripe age of seventy-six, Martha announced her retirement as a dancer, though she continued to choreograph and teach.

Martha had been reluctant to give up her dancing and had a difficult time adjusting to the change. In her words, "I only wanted to dance. Without dancing I wished to die."

Fortunately, Martha stuck it out for two more decades, teaching and creating innovative dances until her death at ninety-six. More than three-fourths of Martha's dancers have become choreographers and directors of dance companies, thus carrying on the influence of perhaps the most powerful and dangerous woman in dance.

Martha's penchant for breaking the rules of dance was inspired by her early training with **Ruth St. Denis** at the Denishawn Dance Company. St. Denis had caused her own share of scandals during her career, by creating dances that incorporated many different cultures, and which embraced female sensuality.

The Women of the
Harlem Renaissance

What the Parisian modern art movement was to Europe, the *Harlem Renaissance* was to 1920s America. New ideas and breakthrough theories were every-where—in the cafés where artists argued all night, in the literary salons where intellectuals held court, and even in the smoky nightclubs where blues musicians experimented with a crazy new sound called **Jazz.**

"Mama exhorted her children to 'jump at de sun.' We might not land on the sun, but at least we got off the ground."

—Zora Neale Hurston

If you had been lucky enough to sit in on any of the café gatherings or artsy dinner parties of the Harlem Renaissance chances are you would have found *Zora Neale Hurston* at the head of the table. Zora embodied everything that was exciting about the movement—she was brilliant, beautiful, and ahead of her time on all counts.

Zora loved to challenge the status quo, and became famous for her studies of black culture, and in particular for her work that debunked dim-witted ideas about white superiority. Trained as an anthropologist, she traveled all over the country to gather research for her work, and gained a reputation for being an astute observer of Americana.

But Zora is best known for the novels that she wrote; her works today are considered to be some of the most important contributions to American fiction. During an era of literature that was dominated by men, Zora's novels stood out as magnificent commentary on the experience of the black American.

Despite her early fame, Zora drifted in the last years of her life, and died in a state of relative obscurity. Her works are now being rediscovered by Americans everywhere, but perhaps the most eloquent tribute to her life was made by author Alice Walker, who, after finding that Hurston had been buried in an unmarked grave, paid to have a headstone placed at the site. It read, simply, *"Genius of the South."*

Some of Zora's masterpieces—

Their Eyes Were Watching God (1937)
Mules and Men (1935)
Dust Tracks on a Road (1942)

Just as the smart set gathered in the salons of Paris, so did the Harlem intelligentsia in America. One of the most famous literary salons was that held by A'Leila Walker (Madame C. J. Walker's daughter—see er profile). Black ntellectuals from ll over the world came to trade ideas and take part in the magic of the Harlem enaissance. They nicknamed her gathering the "Dark Tower."

After she married and became Nella Larsen Imes, she often used the pseudonym Allen Semi, which was her married name reversed.

What happened to Nella Larsen?

The other great female voice of the Harlem Renaissance was *Nella Larsen*, who contributed two of the most important novels to the movement. *Quicksand* and *Passing* have become American classics, and *Quicksand* in particular was hailed as a fresh take on racial identity. Nella was celebrated as a bright new star of American literature, on her way to even greater acclaim. And that's when she disappeared.

That's right—just as quickly as she had burst onto the literary scene, she dropped out. Nella gave up her writing, moved to Europe, then to Brooklyn, and reportedly spent her remaining days as a nurse. While some critics believe that her talent was simply too limited to sustain a literary career, it is doubtful that two such important works could have been flukes.

Whatever her reasons for retiring, Nella had the satisfaction of knowing that she had been at the forefront of one of the most exciting moments in American history. The Harlem Renaissance changed it all, including attitudes about art, modern culture, and even race. Most historians agree that the movement lost steam after the 1920s, but its mark on the cultural landscape was permanent—America had been hurled into the twentieth century, almost despite itself, and now there was no going back.

QUICKSAND

Nella Larsen

Passing

Nella Larsen

Rediscover Nella Larsen today!

Quicksand (1928)

Passing (1929)

Hollywood Power Players

> *"There is nothing connected with the staging of a motion picture that a woman cannot do as easily as a man."*
>
> —ALICE GUY BLANCHÉ

Imagine Hollywood as a company town with WOMEN in all the seats of power—behind the cameras, at the writer's desks, and heading up the deal-making meetings that shape the industry. Imagine a Hollywood where women are shouting from the director's chair, approving the scripts, and running the studios. Imagine that scene and you've got a pretty good idea of the real Hollywood not so long ago—when THE GIRLS RAN THE SHOW.

The Directors

Women directors were a powerful part of early Hollywood—in fact, more so than even today. The most well-known director was **Lois Weber,** who made her mark with bold ideas and controversial subject matter. She was hailed as the "greatest woman director" by Movie Picture Studios, and for a time pulled down the spectacular salary of $5,000 a week. Weber eventually started her own studio in Hollywood. She was such a popular and influential figure at Universal Studios that she was elected mayor of Universal City in 1913.

Sadly, women directors became less prevalent after the 1920s and 1930s. As the movie business became more "respectable," women found it more difficult to find the freedom they had enjoyed in Hollywood's earlier years. Men directed almost every movie to come out of Tinsel Town for decades. A notable exception was **Ida Lupino,** who made the transition from acting to directing during the 1940s. Lupino said she had grown tired of standing around while "someone else seemed to be doing all the interesting work." Like her predecessor Lois Weber, Lupino was famous for taking on tough subjects like unwed motherhood and polio. She was also well known for the power she wielded on her set—and the distinctly motherly manner in which used it. The back of her director's chair read "Mother of Us All."

Ida Lupino

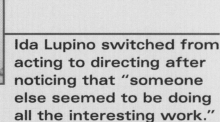

Ida Lupino switched from acting to directing after noticing that "someone else seemed to be doing all the interesting work."

Mary Pickford

THAT'S RIGHT. Even though today most positions of power in Hollywood e filled by men, in its earliest days, women were often in charge. Remember— ese were the days of the "silents," and the fledgling movie industry allowed all pes of people to pursue their dreams. This boomtown mentality left the doors ide open for women who recognized the career potential in this new medium.

Some say that **Alice Guy Blanché,** in essence, created the French cinema. In fact, nearly every movie made by the French production house Gaumont from 1900 to 1905 was directed by her, and she hired all of the men who helped out. Blanché was at the forefront of the introduction of the "talkie," directing more than one hundred in 1906 and 1907 using Gaumont's new "cronophone." In the United States, she supervised the direction of *another* three hundred movies through her own production company. She was widely known for her dislike of melodramatic acting, and had a large sign hung in her studio that encouraged her actors to "BE NATURAL."

Anita Loos

Douglas Fairbanks   John Emerson

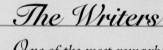

Frances Marion

The Writers

One of the most remarkable women to answer the call of new Hollywood was Frances Marion —easily the most influential screenwriter of the silent era. As a matter of fact, she wrote more than 350 "flickers," prompting many to suggest that Frances Marion basically WAS the movie industry for a time. Marion was the well-kept secret behind the most powerful studios, and one of the highest paid women in the industry—making a salary that was on par with the biggest stars. Other powerful writers included Anita Loos, who was famous for witty, sophisticated comedies that packed the movie houses, including the hugely popular Gentlemen Prefer Blondes. Dorothy Parker (see her separate profile) even did a brief tour of duty as a screenwriter in Hollywood during the 1930s.

Isabella of Castille

Renaissance Queen

Most famous for being the brains behind the brawn of Chris Columbus, Queen Isabella was more than just a royal muse with a big purse. While sponsoring the founding of a new world, Isabella was also busy fighting civil wars, advancing the arts and sciences, and creating a country called Spain.

Spain was a mess before Isabella came along, split into three feuding factions—Castille, Aragon, and Granada. Isabella's mission was to unify Spain into one powerful province—and she pulled this off with surprising finesse.

As daughter of the King of Castille, Isabella's first step was to secretly marry Ferdinand, heir to the throne of Aragon, and thus bring together two of the discordant territories. But rather than inspiring royal rejoicing, Isabella found that her deft diplomacy instigated a royal snit-fit among her Castillian relatives. Her brother Enrique—who was king at the time—had arranged a different marriage for her and resented the audacity of her choosing her own husband. His response was to disown her.

Isabella was hardly one to be bossed around by her brother—king or not—and she threatened him with war. The siblings' royal rivalry continued until Enrique died five years later, without having designated an heir. Isabella promptly had herself declared Queen of Castille, but Enrique's daughter put up a ferocious fight. After years of civil war, Isabella finally gained the crown.

Her queenship secured, Isabella saw her husband crowned King of Aragon soon afterwards, and next she set her sights on the Moorish stronghold of Granada. But here her story takes a turn for the unsavory . . .

Isabella was the first female monarch in Spain for whom the hallowed "sword of justice" was carried at the coronation ceremony.

Isabella felt certain that religious unity was crucial to a cohesive nation, so she banned all religions other than her beloved Roman Catholicism. Ferdinand agreed with her extremist stance, and their fanatacism led to the Spanish Inquisition in which all non-Christians were forced to convert or leave Spain. An estimated two thousand people died as a result of this "religious cleansing" and thousands more were driven from their homes. After eleven years of this dirty campaign, "the Catholic Kings" succeeded in winning Granada, and thus Spain was united for the first time in eight hundred years. The lives and liberties of some of the country's greatest citizens, however, was a high price to pay for this achievement.

Fortunately, Isabella was more open-minded in other areas. When Columbus brought Native Americans back to Spain to serve as slaves, Isabella, who fiercely opposed slavery, ordered their release. She was also a patron and collector of Spanish and Flemish art, a big supporter of the sciences, and many books of that time were dedicated to her.

As queen, Isabella studied Latin—the language of diplomacy—and the knightly fighting arts, in an attempt to make up for not having a monarch's formal training. Considered a great military genius, Isabella also planned and supervised battles and did hard time in the field, even when she was pregnant. No shrinking violet, Isabella is also said to have stood up to the Pope on a number of occasions when she disapproved of his appointments.

When Isabella's troops went to battle, she was usually right alongside them—decked out in armor, mounted on her horse, and urging the soldiers on.

Joan *of* Arc

Joan of Arc was the most spectacular thing to hit Europe—prior or since. At the age of seventeen, Joan left her small village in France, donned man's clothing, and rode out to save her country. She established herself as one of the greatest warriors of all time by doing what countless male soldiers, infantrymen, and kings had found impossible—liberating her beloved France.

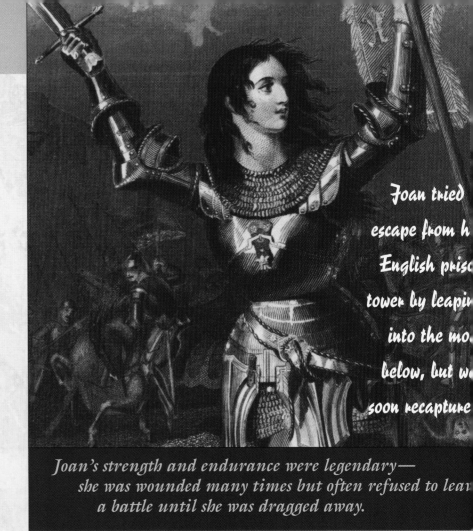

Joan tried
escape from h
English prisc
tower by leapi
into the mo
below, but w
soon recapture

*Joan's strength and endurance were legendary—
she was wounded many times but often refused to leav
a battle until she was dragged away.*

When Joan of Arc was born in 1412, France was a defeated, despondent country. The English had occupied the nation for many years, and the French people—without a king or any effective leadership—were powerless to drive them out.

But while the Frenchmen in command had been arguing amongst themselves and generally proving to be useless, Joan d'Arc had been growing up a pious and headstrong girl in the small town of Domremy. When she was about twelve, she began hearing voices—of the saints, she said—who told her that if anyone was going to save her country, it would have to be her.

At age seventeen, Joan decided that her voices were right. She made her way to Charles VII, the would-be king of France—and persuaded him to give her a chance. Once convinced of Joan's divine powers, Charles made her a captain, equipped her with troops, and sent her off to win back the township of Orleans from the English. This was a nearly impossible objective—the French forces were hopelessly outnumbered, and had all but given up hope of defending the city.

And that's when Joan rode in, assessed the situation, and delivered the most stunning military success of the century. With a combination of cool-headed leadership and breathtaking bravery, Joan literally ran the English out of town. Her victory stunned Charles and his military leaders, and many called it a miracle.

Orleans would be the first of many "miraculous" successes. Joan spent the next year winning more battles and liberating more cities, and finally succeeded in seeing Charles VII crowned as the King of France.

Joan's career as France's most famous soldier was shortlived—only a year after her victory at Orleans, she was captured by the English. Her bravery in captivity was just as fantastic as it had been in war. Kept in chains and interrogated relentlessly, Joan eventually became weak and sick to the point of near-death. Her captors recognized the significance of her spirituality and were particularly intent on forcing her to deny her relationship to the saints.

But Joan refused to recant her beliefs, saying that no amount of torture would make her deny her personal relationship with the saints. She was also stubbornly defiant about her right to wear men's clothing, claiming that she would always wear a soldier's uniform if called to defend her country. This final statement, which was considered heretical, was used to condemn her to execution. Joan was burned at the stake. During the ordeal, she asked a Dominican monk to hold high a cross and shout the assurances of salvation so that she could hear them above the roar of the flames. As she burned, a white dove was said to have flown out of the fire toward her beloved France.

Although a great warrior, Joan is also remembered for her generosity to the poor and other acts of selfless charity. This sensitivity did not leave her on the battlefield, where she wept bitterly at the death of her enemies and the violence of war.

The executioners' attempt to disgrace Joan had exactly the opposite effect. Her sentence was revoked twenty years later, and she was made a saint in 1920. She is still the most popular, beloved figure in French history, and May 30th is a national holiday in her honor.

Lakshmi Bai The Rani of Jhansi

Hell hath no fury like that of a warrior queen, especially when called on to defend her country. The British learned this lesson the hard way, when they seized the beloved homeland of the Rani of Jhansi, Lakshmi Bai. She emerged as one of India's greatest warriors, and is now revered as one of the most valiant military leaders of the famous Great Rebellion.

LAKSHMI BAI—or "Little Manu" as she was called as a girl—was born around 1830 in Benares, India, into a life of relative privilege. Her father was an important political advisor, and so she was afforded opportunities unavailable to most young girls during the time. She was trained in nearly every sporting activity, including fencing, the martial arts, and horsemanship. She was also given a vigorous academic preparation—equally unusual for the time. Manu's destiny seems to have been set from the start, and indeed the legend has it that her horoscope predicted a powerful position in her future.

That destiny was fulfilled when she was married to the Raja of Jhansi, the highest ruler of the Indian region of Jhansi. It was at this time that she took the name of Lakshmi Bai, and became the Rani of Jhansi. (In India, a Rani is the rough equivalent of a queen, and Raja of a king.) They adopted a son when they did not produce an heir, and when the Raja died after ten years of marriage, the Rani assumed that she would rule along with her son.

But the British were the occupying force in India at the time, and they suddenly announced that they would not recognize the Rani's son as a rightful heir, and instead would annex the region of Jhansi as their own. The Indian citizens were stunned, as the Rani had shown herself to be one of the most capable leaders in their history. She was well known as a shrewd negotiator, and rose at three A.M. on most mornings to begin her duties. The Rani was heartbroken but felt helpless, and is said to have cried out "I will not give up my Jhansi."

Lakshmi suffered this situation for four years before she was given the chance to act. The Indians had begun to organize the Great Rebellion of 1857, and the Rani decided to help them in their uprising.

> "Little Manu" was amazingly brave even as a girl. One story tells of the day that a wild elephant charged her when she was only seven years old. She stood absolutely still until it was near enough for her to jump onto one of its tusks, from where she was able to calm the animal.

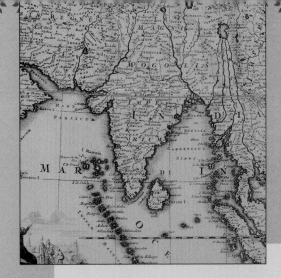

Lakshmi Bai's natural leadership abilities and aptitude for military strategy quickly made her one of its key military advisors. She helped organize the defense of the main fortress of Jhansi, and in the British siege that followed, she fought valiantly alongside her men.

Lakshmi was visible during the entire battle to both sides, with her flag flying high. When the Indian defense appeared to be hopeless, the Rani escaped with four of her followers. She began riding for the nearby fortress of Kalpi under hot pursuit by the British. But her stamina and horsemanship skills served her well, and she outran her pursuers, covering more than one hundred miles in only a day.

From there she strategized with other Indian leaders, and eventually planned a daring maneuver—she and her forces would attempt to win back the Gwalior fortress from the British. Their plan was a success, and the Rani was honored for her role with a beautiful pearl necklace from the treasury of Gwalior.

But the British soon came back to reclaim their captured fortress, and another great battle ensued. Once again, the Rani was in the midst of the fighting, but this time she did not survive. She died alongside her men, in full armor and her symbolic necklace. She was twenty-two years old.

The famous Rani of Jhansi has since become one of India's most revered heros. The history books are filled with accounts of her bravery, and even the British acknowledged her heroism, as in this written remark from Sir Hugh Rose: "In her death the rebels lost their bravest and best military leader." But her true legend lives on in the form of countless ballads, songs, and stories in Indian culture.

Lakshmi was a brilliant horsewoman, and was known to maneuver her mount with her reins in her teeth and a sword in each hand.

The Rani trained a small army of women to help defend the main fortress during the battles with the British.

In court, the Rani wore an ensemble that was fit for a queen *and* warrior. She combined a turban and diamond bangles with a sword and two silver pistols.

LOZEN, Apache Warrior

Riding in an Apache war party must have been the wildest kind of rush — whooping at the top of your lungs, galloping at full speed, and somehow forgetting that every breath you take may be your last. Imagine, if you can, that kind of feeling, and you've got a window into the soul of one of the greatest female fighters of all time — Lozen, the bravest Apache maiden.

Under the brutal laws of warfare that governed the plains of North America during the 1800s, no warriors were more feared and respected than the Apaches. Their reputation for courage and skill on the battlefield was renowned across the cultures of other tribes, as well as by the new white settlers. The stories of leaders like Geronimo fill the pages of American history books and Apache legend, but few know the tale of the Apache woman who fought bravely at the side of the men, and rose to become one of the greatest leaders of the tribe.

Lozen was the sister of another great Apache leader, Victorio. In this position of relative stature, she was given more freedom than many of the other Apache women to pursue her tomboyish activities. As a girl, Lozen learned to ride and rope as well as any of the men, and she soon gained the reputation as the best horse-handler in the tribe. It was this skill that made Lozen so valuable in battle. One of the most important objectives of the Apache raids was to steal the horses of the enemy, and Lozen was a master at stampeding and capturing the panicked animals during the heat of battle.

Lozen gained stature with every outing, as she performed valiantly in raid after raid, nearly always bringing home the highly-prized horses of the enemy camp. Off the battlefield, she

Lozen was one of the two messengers sent by **Geronimo** to negotiate his final surrender.

The Suffragists (see their separate profile) were highly impressed with the system of female leadership used by the Iroquois tribes in New York. The Native American women were shocked to find that the rights of white women were nearly non-existent compared to their own.

also became respected as a loyal protector of her people. One legend tells of the time that she was stranded with a young mother and child in enemy territory, and, rather than ride away to safety, spent months guarding the pair and leading them back to safer soil. As Lozen aged, she became an acknowledged leader of the tribe, and her opinion was particularly respected in matters related to upcoming battle plans.

But fighting women were not exclusive to the Apaches.
The Cherokees tell of the legendary **Ehyophsta,** otherwise known as **Yellow Haired Woman,** who fought fearlessly in battle against an attack by Shoshonis in 1869. She was

originally hidden in the tents with the rest of the women, but she grew so incensed during the attack that she ran out to join the battle. Ehyophsta rode into the thick of the fighting on her horse with only her butcher knife, and killed one of the attackers single-handedly. And in the 1600s, the Eastern-coast Wampanoag tribe boasted of the fearless **Wetamoo**— also known as the **Squaw Sachem**—who led her people in a fight against the British colonialists. She waged a brave battle against the invaders, leading three hundred warriors in attacks against their various towns along the coast, but was ultimately defeated by their overwhelming forces.

The Forgotten First Girl Scout

When explorers Lewis and Clark made their famous trek across the Americas, they were under the sure-footed direction of girl-guide **Sacajawea.** But while the famous explorers made the history books, Sacajawea—who traveled just as far, and with a baby on her back—barely got a mention.

Mother Jones

JOIN THE UNION, BOYS!

If you'd been present at one of the many violent miners' strikes that erupted during the late 1800s, you probably would have seen Mother Jones at the head of the crowd shouting those exact words. It must have been an amazing sight—a small, grandmotherly woman suddenly coming alive to fire up the proceedings with an explosive mix of passion and eloquence. She was a glorious study in contrasts, Mother Jones, meaning that the little granny who seemed the picture of innocence was actually, for a time, branded

"The most dangerous woman in America."

Mary Harris Jones was born with revolution in her blood. She grew up in Ireland, where her grandfather was hanged for his efforts to obtain Ireland's independence from the Brits. She came to America after her father was forced to flee the country for those same beliefs.

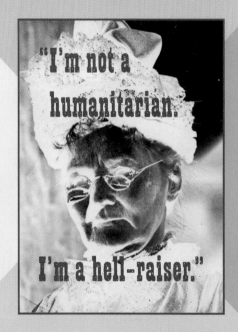

"I'm not a humanitarian. I'm a hell-raiser."

for most of her years as a union agitator, Mother Jones had no home. She lived as a kind of pilgrim of the poor, staying in the homes of union sympathizers, and depending on their hospitality for sustenance. In her words: **"My address is like my shoes. It travels with me. I abide where there is a fight against wrong."**

One of the cooler things about Mother Jones was that she continued to fight well into her latest years. She was jailed many times in her eighties, and was still leading movements during her nineties. Some historians speculate that her elderly appearance gave her a considerable advantage—after all, how could you beat up a ninety-year-old woman?

What fueled the fires of Mother Jones' passion?

Her own rock-solid beliefs, certainly, and probably two tragedies that marked her earlier years. In 1867, while living in Memphis, she lost her entire family—her husband and four children—to an epidemic of yellow fever. It was the kind of catastrophe that would have broken most people, but Jones somehow managed to carry on. She moved to Chicago and had begun to work for the wealthy as a seamstress, when she was again struck by the cruel hand of fate. When the Great Chicago Fire of 1871 swept the city, she lost everything.

It was through these devastating experiences that Jones began to develop a righteous and deep-seated anger about the plight of the working class. In her words, she had seen the *"jobless and the hungry, walking alongside the frozen lakefront . . . My employers seemed neither to notice or care."*

The Great Fire brought her to the union movement. She turned to the unions for aid and was attracted to their crusade to improve the life of the working classes. Mother Jones decided to join their fight.

AND WITH THAT DECISION was born one of the most effective labor leaders of all time. It is said that she could single-handedly keep a strike alive with her rhetoric. This talent made her famous within the unions, and despised by the strikebreaking companies they were fighting. The authorities began to target her for arrest, and she was thrown in jail too many times to count—even when she was in her eighties.

The strikes were often violent, with the government sometimes firing on the workers, but Mother Jones was unfazed. She was also an expert at organizing the wives of the strikers, and would tell the women to bring their babies with them when they were arrested. She told them to sing all night, and to let their babies cry. It drove the jailers crazy, and they could hardly wait to set the women free.

Mother Jones also worked tirelessly for the rights of children—many of whom were exploited in factories during her day. In 1903, she led a movement in Philadelphia against the abuse of children in the textile factories. *"Philadelphia's mansions were built on the broken bones, the quivering hearts and drooping heads of these children,"* she said in one of her most famous speeches.

Well into her nineties, Mother Jones was fighting for the rights of garment, steel, and streetcar workers. On her one-hundredth birthday, officials and luminaries from all over the country paid their respects, including John D. Rockefeller, whose father she had fought against in many strikes.

Today, she is considered to be a heroine of the working classes. If the poor or the disadvantaged have a **protecting saint, she might very well be seen in the stormy face of Mother Jones.**

The little granny who seemed the picture of innocence was actually branded "the most dangerous woman in America."

Shirley Muldowney
Racing Ace Supreme

Sitting inside of a machine going 300 M.P.H. is more like being part of a bomb than driving a car. When the start gun fires, you don't accelerate—you explode. For most of us, it's a stretch to imagine surviving that kind of speed, much less controlling it. But then most of us aren't Shirley Muldowney— **the reigning** *Queen of the Raceways.*

Shirley was a sucker for speed from her early days in high school, where she began muscling out the hometown boys in street races in Schenectady, New York. From there she moved into the rough-and-tumble world of 1960s drag racing, where she made her mark as one of the best drivers in the field. It was there that she acquired her trademark handle of "Cha-Cha" and began to gain fame as the only prominent woman in the most masculine of sports.

Shirley endured this image as the femme fatale of racing until a close call in 1973 changed her attitude. She knew that the sport was too serious—and potentially too deadly—for such theatrics. She retired her nickname of Cha-Cha, and encouraged female racers to concentrate on the sport rather than their gender, saying: **"THERE'S NO ROOM FOR BIMBOISM IN DRAG RACING."**

"I drove them when they were really bad machines."

—S. M. on the "Funny Cars" that she drove in the 1970s— notorious for their unpredictable power and tendency to catch fire.

She moved up through the ranks of speed classes, finally qualifying for the "Top Fuel" dragsters that are the fastest earth-bound machines in the world. Some observers were skeptical about her ability to compete at this new level, and speculated that Shirley was more of a curiosity than a real threat. These doubts she dispelled almost immediately, as she broke records, won races, and generally racked up one of the most awesome track records in the history of racing.

When Shirley won the world championship in 1977, her fame spread beyond the racing world to the general public. Everyone was talking about the fastest woman on earth; the one who had smashed every barrier in the boys-only world of racing. In 1982, she won the championship at the U.S. Nationals, the achievement of which she is most proud.

I n 1984, it all stopped. At a speed of 250 M.P.H., Shirley had a crash that ended her career for nearly two years, and very nearly ended her life. She was badly injured, with both legs severely crippled, and went through five major surgeries to save them. It was the kind of experience that would keep the bravest driver from climbing behind a wheel again. Most fans assumed that Shirley Muldowney would never return to the sport.

They were wrong. After eighteen grueling months of rehabilitation, Shirley roared back into the race world with a vengeance, and was soon racking up titles again. It was an incredible comeback, and the media went wild. Everybody wanted to cover Shirley's story, and she ended up on magazines, newspapers, and even the *Tonight Show* with Johnny Carson.

The acknowledged "queen of speed" hasn't stopped since. She is arguably the most recognized driver of her time, having won more championships, awards, and titles than she can count. In 1989, she became one of only a few drivers in the world to enter the "Four Second Club," meaning that she covered a quarter-mile in less than five seconds. In case you're wondering how fast that is, let's just say—*IT'S FAST.*

In 1998, Shirley will have been racing for forty years, and at fifty-seven years old, she has no intention of slowing down—on or off the track. She's still racing with the tops in the field, and was voted to the All-American team in 1996, for a total of six times. When she was inducted into the Motorsport Hall of Fame, some observers wondered if she would be happy to retire. Don't count on it. Shirley said simply, "I'm still ready to wax some tails."

Who can argue with that?

Shirley marks her proudest moment as the day that she won the championship at the U.S. Nationals. Not only was she the only woman to have ever done so, she recorded the fastest time in the history of the race.

Shirley couldn't resist the invitation to ride in an F-18 jet fighter in 1988. She handled the 750 M.P.H. G-Force experience like the pro she is, later saying: "It was the most exciting ride I've ever taken."

"If you want something bad enough there are ways to do it. But you've got to stand your ground—if not they will walk on you like an old shoe." —S. M.

Want More on Shirley and Other Racing Women?
- See *Heart Like a Wheel* (1984) The story of Shirley's life, starring Bonnie Bedelia and Beau Bridges
- Or check out Shirley's web site at www.shirleymuldowney.com

Queen Njinga African Ruler

On the day that Queen Njinga arrived to negotiate with the Portuguese colonialists who had just invaded her land, the colonialists believed they clearly had the upper hand. After all, here was a leader from a backward civilization, coming from a position of little power. But most importantly, she was a woman, and surely would be easily cheated. Of course, they had never dealt with a woman like Queen Njinga.

As legend has it, Njinga—sister of the Angolan king—was dispatched as a royal diplomat to deal with the Portuguese. When Njinga arrived at the meeting, she found that all the seats were taken—by men. She shrewdly recognized a very conscious oversight on the part of her adversaries. They hoped to undermine her authority and self-confidence with the symbolism of the forgotten chair.

The Portuguese underestimated Njinga big time. She coolly ordered a member of her entourage to kneel, and proceeded to make herself comfortable seated on his back. It was Njinga's first political outing, and she had shown, with one gesture, exactly who was in charge.

Queen Njinga (pronounced NIN-JA) was born in Angola on the western coast of Africa in 1582. Then, as now, Africa was a complicated, chaotic continent. When the Europeans arrived, they thought they had found the promised land—a paradise theirs for the taking. Kingdoms sprung up quickly, borders and flags changed often, and governing regimes shifted like the desert sands. Only the most powerful personalities were able to successfully navigate the uncertain political terrain. To be effective, a monarch had to be sophisticated, intelligent, and occasionally ruthless—no ruler rose to the challenge better than Queen Njinga.

Although Njinga preferred fighting her battles at the negotiating table, she didn't run from physical conflict when it couldn't be avoided. During times of outright war, she proved herself an accomplished military strategist and waged many successful campaigns against her European opponents.

Dressed in animal skins, a sword hanging from her neck, and an ax around her waist, Queen Njinga looked like a ruler, and exuded power and confidence. In an attempt to unify her land, and strengthen her political position, Njinga sharpened her spears and conquered several tribes near her own.

Njinga had a social conscience too. Although her birthright gave her considerable influence from the start, she did not become Queen of Angola until her brother's death in 1624, when she was forty-two. And once she made it to the top, Queen Njinga gave other women (including her two sisters) a boost—she filled the highest positions in her government with female leaders.

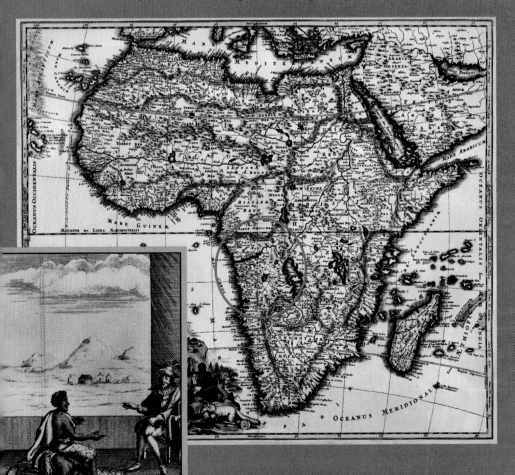

Queen Njinga makes her own seat at the negotiating session with the Portuguese.

A FEW GOOD WOMEN

Centuries ago, in the Sahara, real women carried spears. At least that's what archaeologists have recently learned in their discoveries of ancient drawings of women warriors. These women were so tough that they often served as bodyguards for the leaders of many tribal cultures. They also organized themselves into small armies to protect their homes and families.

As recently as the late 1800s, a kingdom in West Africa was protected by regiments of Amazons—the type of women who gave pause to the bravest of invaders. The all-girl army, made up of five thousand of the toughest females in town, guarded the palace and took part in many battles. This estrogen-powered regiment astonished European visitors. One wrote, "I would prefer these female warriors to the male ones of this country."

63

Annie Oakley

Dubbed **"Little Sure Shot"** by the great Sioux warrior Sitting Bull, Annie Oakley sure was little—about five feet tall and under a hundred pounds—and her shot sure was sure.

Annie was both wholesome and daring, which made her simultaneously reassuring and provocative to her fans. On one hand she was beautiful and primly and properly feminine: She had a traditional, respectable marriage, embroidery was her favorite pastime, and the Bible her favorite book. On the other hand, she wore her hair long and dresses short at a time when Victorian women were more modest in appearance. And Annie brandished a rifle—a potent symbol of manhood—which she was a master at handling. Aware of her paradoxical traits, Annie once referred to herself as "a crack shot in petticoats."

A big crowd-pleaser was Annie's ability to shoot four glass balls before they hit the ground—something that she could also do while standing on the back of a galloping horse.

Annie was very social-minded. In her later years she had her medals melted down, sold the gold, and donated the money to charity. She was also a great believer in the value of education, and helped several female students by financing their studies.

At thirty paces Annie could hit the thin edge of a playing card or a dime tossed in the air. She could blow the end off a cigarette held in her trusting husband's lips and could shoot the flames off candles as they rotated on a wheel.

Annie wows them with her sharpshooting in Philadelphia, 1895.

The Original Cowgirl—Lucy MULHALL

Lucille Mulhall was the only woman of her time to rope competitively with men. Referred to as "America's greatest horsewoman" and "the queen of the range," Lucille earned top spots in contests and vaudeville shows for over twenty years just after the turn of the century.

Paradoxically, this "cowboy girl" was extremely feminine and soft-spoken. She was beautiful enough to become a society belle, but Lucille loved the rough, dangerous life of cowboying and would give it up for nothing. As a child she preferred branding yearlings and roping steer to playing with dolls or sewing. While her sisters participated in typical girly pastimes of the nineteenth century, Lucille was out training ponies and practicing trick riding. By the time she was eight, Lucy was a skilled roper and by her teens the top western performer.

Referred to as a "Lassoer in Lingerie," by journalists trying to describe this woman of mixed abilities, Lucille was rescued from the world of unwieldy witticisms by her friend and admirer Will Rogers. Rogers called her a "cowgirl," thus coining a term and securing Lucille's status as the prototype for one of America's most appealing icons.

Annie gets her gun . . .

Born Phoebe Ann Mosey in 1860, Annie started shooting when she was barely big enough to hold a rifle. Her father died when she was five, leaving her mother with no money and a brood of hungry children. Though the force of her first shot left eight-year-old Annie with a broken nose, she succeeded in hitting her target. In fact, once Annie got her hands on a gun, her family never lacked for food. She could shoot the head off a running quail by the time she was twelve and became a supplier of game birds to hotels as far as a hundred miles away. Hotels paid a premium for meat that was clean of buckshot and Annie consistently hit her prey in the head, leaving the body intact and her family well-cared for.

According to legend, when Annie was twenty-one, a ranking marksman came to town and challenged her to a showdown. Frank E. Butler was satisfied when he hit 21 out of 25 clay pigeons—that is until Annie blasted **23 of 25** out of the sky. Frank gracefully acknowledged her skill—in fact, his admiration was so great that he courted Annie and within a year they were married. Later Frank recalled their first encounter saying, *"I almost dropped dead when a little slim girl in a short dress stepped out . . . never did a person make more impossible shots than that little girl."*

Annie Wows 'em Worldwide

Annie was literally and figuratively a straight shooter. She practiced religiously, refused to use deceptions, and she wouldn't wear makeup. She wowed audiences the world over with such feats as hitting a dime in a man's hand while leaving his fingers intact and hitting a target over her shoulder by viewing its reflection in a knife blade.

In Berlin, Annie obliged Crown Prince Wilhelm (later Kaiser Wilhelm II) by letting him hold a cigarette in his mouth which she shot cleanly. In Europe she gave command performances for the Baroness de Rothchilds and Queen Victoria. When the Wild West show toured Paris, the king of Senegal tried to buy Annie from Buffalo Bill. And the great Sioux leader, Sitting Bull, was so impressed by Annie that he made her his adopted daughter.

When World War I came, Annie was well into her fifties, but she was still shooting away. Turned down by the U.S. War Department when she offered her services as a shooting instructor, she volunteered to entertain the troops with such stunts as shooting an apple off her dog Dave's head.

Scarlett

The Fiercest Southern Belle

Lights! Camera! Atlanta!
Filming the epic of the decade—

- The burning of Atlanta scene was shot on old movie sets, which were burned to clear the back lot of the studio to build Tara.
- It took three weeks to make one striped dress for Scarlett.
- Filming took nearly eleven months in 1939.

One of the most forceful femme fatales to ever hit the big screen, **Scarlett O'Hara** shredded every idea about sweet Southern womanhood in one roof-raising, epic performance. She stole every scene she had in *Gone With the Wind*, reminding audiences that any given magnolia could be a hellcat when provoked.

So what if she was only a character? As one of the most dazzling images of feminine grit in modern history, Scarlett was still an inspiration to millions of women. She was no role model—what with her self-centered ways and sorry treatment of Rhett Butler—but Scarlett O'Hara, as a paragon of feminine power, was a bonified American icon.

Thanks to the smashing success of the book and the movie *Gone With the Wind*, Scarlett O'Hara was also the most famous southern belle in the world. Audiences everywhere appreciated her multifaceted character, warming up to her more admirable qualities—like her tenacity, for instance. Not many people could bounce back after an episode like the burning of Atlanta.

Y'all, she was also brave. When a Yankee deserter broke into her Tara home and threatened her, Scarlett shot him in the head with her father's revolver. (You just don't mess with a woman defending her home.) Another appealing thing about Scarlett is that she did it all in "a man's world." Frankly, she didn't give a damn. She was the kind of woman who could play any hand dealt her—and win. No wonder we love her.

The Women Behind Scarlett

Margaret MITCHELL
"The Little Lady with the Big Book"

There would be no Scarlett O'Hara without Margaret Munnerlyn Mitchell. *Gone With the Wind* was her first and only book. Margaret, an Atlanta debutante, wrote features and an advice column for the local newspaper, until, at twenty-six, she was forced to stay at home while she recovered from an ankle injury. While recuperating, she started writing a little something called *Gone With the Wind*. It took her ten years to finish, but it was worth the wait. Margaret won the Pulitzer Prize for her efforts, and sold 1.5 million copies of her book in its first year. When the movie debuted in 1939, it won ten Academy Awards. Mitchell was dubbed, fittingly, "the little lady with the big book."

Vivien LEIGH
A Star Is Born

Vivien Leigh was as stubborn as Scarlett when it came to winning this part. The search for the perfect Scarlett is Hollywood legend. Casting directors auditioned 1,400 women, including Joan Crawford and Lucille Ball, in their nationwide hunt. Vivien shouldn't have had a chance. She was British, for one thing—a clear disadvantage in the competition to play a genuine Southern belle. And she was a total unknown—remember, every major actress in Hollywood was interested in this plum part, and Vivien was a relative nobody in their midst.

The producers were still searching when filming began. But when Vivien walked onto the set they knew they had finally found their Scarlett O'Hara. The role won her an Academy Award, and made her an instant star.

No Vomiting for Viv
Vivien refused to make the vomiting sounds needed for the scene at the end of Part One, so Olivia de Haviland did it.

More GWTW Trivia
- Turns out Vivien Leigh began reading *GWTW* while recovering from an ankle injury.
- Originally, Margaret Mitchell named the main character in her book Pansy O'Hara.

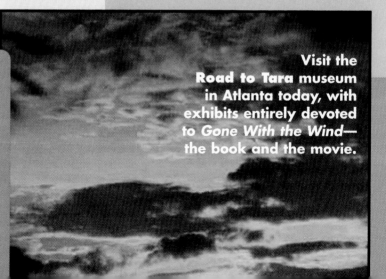

Visit the **Road to Tara** museum in Atlanta today, with exhibits entirely devoted to *Gone With the Wind*— the book and the movie.

Or revisit the original! Buy the *GWTW* book or rent the movie—it's a story that never gets old.

Georgia O'Keeffe
THE RENEGADE ARTIST

One of the greatest artists of the twentieth century, Georgia O'Keeffe challenged notions of style, theory, and possibility when she emerged on the modern art scene. In her day, women were sorely underrepresented in the male-dominated art world, but that didn't stop Georgia from painting her way to becoming an American legend.

One of Georgia's trailblazing techniques was breaking down an object into "pieces" to get at its essence. By painting familiar objects — like flowers — in intense close-up, Georgia made them unfamiliar and interesting.

68

"At last, a woman on paper!" exclaimed Alfred Stieglitz upon seeing Georgia O'Keeffe's drawings in 1916. Alfred, the director of "291," a hot New York City gallery, displayed what he called the "purest, finest, sincerest things that have entered 291 in a long while," and thus launched the career of one of the greatest American artists.

Georgia was born to be an artist, and knew it from the time she was eight years old. As a child on her parents' farm in Wisconsin, Georgia declared her calling and began taking lessons. She took off for serious training in Chicago at eighteen and moved on to New York two years later. There she studied at the reputable Art Students League, but the pressure to conform to what other artists— like Cezanne, Picasso, and the American realists—were doing was discouraging to Georgia. She knew her vision was different, and rather than compromise it, she quit painting and took up commercial art.

Fortunately, Georgia eventually found the support she craved—first from an instructor at Columbia University named Arthur Dove, and later from Alfred Stieglitz, who recognized the quality and originality of her work. Alfred fearlessly exhibited Georgia's paintings despite the stir they caused.

Once Georgia was free to paint by her own instincts, there was no stopping her. **Her first show caused a sensation.** The gallery was filled with critics and other spectators curious to see the works of the controversial woman artist. Alfred reveled in the uproar they caused. Georgia

Georgia was an independent spirit in every way. She learned to drive at a time when few women did, bought a car, and converted the back seat to a studio so she could paint wherever she pleased. Not a particularly safe driver, she'd high-tail it out into the desert looking for subjects to paint—usually flowers, bones, or landscapes.

"The meaning of a word to me is not so exact as the meaning of a color."

knew she had finally *"strip[ped] away what I had been taught— to accept as true my own thinking."* It was this "truth" in her work that Alfred, critics, and other art patrons were so moved by.

In 1929, Georgia traveled to New Mexico and hence began her love affair with the American Southwest. Georgia would become most famous for her painting of desert landscapes and objects. Among them were close-ups of flowers and animal bones, stark depictions of adobe buildings, and organic renderings of sprawling mountains.

Georgia divided her time between New Mexico and New York, where she lived with Alfred (whom she had married in 1924). Alfred refused to leave the Northeast, and Georgia couldn't compromise her calling, so she went to the desert solo.

Soon after Alfred died, she moved to her beloved New Mexico full-time.

Georgia had a house in a town called Abiquiu and would often retreat to her "Ghost Ranch" to paint without distraction for days on end. She also took advantage of her later years to travel abroad. A series from this period features ethereal paintings of clouds as seen from her airplane window.

Having created more than nine hundred works during her lifetime, Georgia died at the age of ninety-eight. Her art is preserved in books, museums, and galleries. A collection of about five hundred photographs of her, taken by Alfred, also remains, capturing many dimensions of perhaps the most wonderful and interesting female artist of all time.

Are YOU a Renegade Artist?

- For more on Georgia, write to:
  Georgia O'Keeffe Museum
  217 Johnson Street
  Santa Fe, NM 87501

- Or contact your local museum to find out what programs they have for kids and young adults.

Dorothy Parker

As the wittiest member of the smart set, Dorothy Parker embodied everything that was glamorous, smart, and sparkling about New York in the 1920s. As part of the inner circle of the famed Algonquin Round Table, she traded wisecracks and opinions with the sharpest literary minds of the day, making her nearly as famous for her witticisms as she was for her writing.

As the brilliant and caustic poster girl for the literati, there's no doubt that **Dorothy Parker** had more influence on her generation than any other woman of her time. As a satirical poet, author, short-story writer, critic, screenwriter, and *bon vivant*, Parker captured the essence of American women's burgeoning freedoms—and also its angst.

The Fabulous Flappers of the 20s

The 1920s were defined by the "flapper" spirit, which meant plenty of fun, freedom, and fast living. Women were cutting loose with their new-found liberty; drinking and smoking in public, "bobbing" their hair short, and even wearing "short" calf-length dresses. In one remarkable decade, American women dropped their Victorian pasts in the dust; their motto was "Anything goes," and they meant it.

This new attitude led many conservatives to believe that civilization was coming to an end. But in fact, it was just beginning and Dorothy Parker's words gave meaning to a complex and emotionally difficult time. Her verses, which caught the country's elite, so-called sophisticates by storm were considered brusque, bitter, and unwomanly by her detractors. And they were.

Although a romantic in many ways, Parker was better known for her devastating cynicism, always couched in the most clever of word-work. Responsible for the famous line, "Men seldom make passes at girls who wear glasses," Parker made a name for herself as the drama critic for *Vanity Fair*. (She was fired for her sharp-tongued reviews and once dryly noted that Katharine Hepburn "ran the gamut of emotions from A to B.") She went on to write book reviews for the *New Yorker*, all the while working on her own short stories and poems. Her most famous story "The Big Blonde," won the prestigious O. Henry Award in 1929.

Dorothy Goes Hollywood

In 1933, Parker took off to claim fame in Hollywood and ended up collaborating on such movies as *A Star is Born* (with Janet Gaynor not Streisand). She wrote book reviews for *Esquire* magazine and worked on some plays. While respected by most, Mrs. Parker was considered a loose cannon by others and (fortunately) found herself on the outskirts of the Hollywood community during its communist witch-hunting era.

The Algonguin Round Table— The Smartest Set

Perhaps the most popular of Dorothy Parker's achievements was her participation in the **Algonquin Round Table,** an informal group of American literary men and women who met daily for lunch at a large, round table in New York City's elegant Algonquin Hotel. The intimate group of artistic buddies began meeting in 1919, and within just a couple of years its chairs were occupied by some of the most famous writers and artists in the city.

While the gaiety thrived during the 1920s, its members gradually went their separate ways, and the last meeting of the Round Table took place in 1943.

Check out the movie *Mrs. Parker and the Vicious Circle* (1995), if you want to see one version of Dorothy's life played out on screen.

The Poet

The Wit
"I don't care what is written about me so long as it isn't true."

A single flow'r he sent me, since we met.
    All tenderly his messenger he chose;
Deep-hearted, pure, with scented dew still wet—
    One perfect rose.

I knew the language of the floweret;
    "My fragile leaves," it said, "his heart enclose."
Love long has taken for his amulet
    One perfect rose.

The Critic
"This is not a novel to be tossed aside lightly. It should be thrown aside with great force."

Why is it no one ever sent me yet
    One perfect limousine, do you suppose?

—"One Perfect Rose"

Lady Pirates

Sure, we all know about Bluebeard, Blackbeard, and Kidd, but few people realize that two of the toughest pirates to ever sail the seas were women. Swashbuckling, crafty, and fearless—the bad girls of the high seas were just as daring as the men who fought by their side.

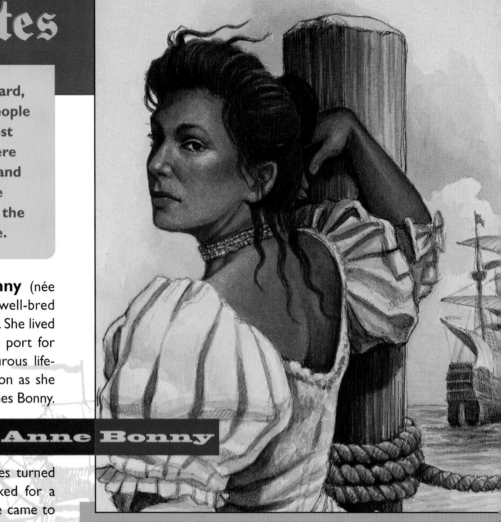

Anne Bonny

orn around 1700, **Anne Bonny** (née Cormac) was raised as the well-bred daughter of a prominent attorney. She lived in Charleston, South Carolina, a popular port for pirates. Anne was drawn to the adventurous lifestyle of piracy from an early age and, soon as she could, married the rogue pirate-sailor James Bonny.

When James tried to steal Anne's father's plantation, Dad disowned the luckless newlyweds and they set off for the Bahamas. There James turned stool pigeon, ratting on sailors he disliked for a reward by saying they were pirates. Anne came to dislike her spineless husband.

It wasn't long before our woman of the seas captivated the imagination of Captain Calico Jack Rackham (who, legend says, created the pirates' skull and crossbones symbol). At that time a wife could be sold at public auction to the highest bidder as long as both parties agreed, so Calico Jack offered to buy Anne from James. James brought the matter to the governor who determined that instead, Anne should be returned to her husband and whipped. That night, Calico Jack and Anne slipped into the harbor, stole a sloop, and set sail for a life of piracy.

WHEN THE CHIPS ARE DOWN

hen Mary and Anne's ship was captured, many of the crew were drunk and fled below deck. Mary and Anne stayed above—fighting. Periodically they'd call to the shipmates to come up and defend the ship.

"If there's a man among ye, ye'll come out and fight like the men ye are to be!" shouted Anne. *"Dogs! Instead of these weaklings, if I only had some women with me."*

When their command was ignored, Anne and Mary fired into the hold, killing one man and wounding several.

Later, when Anne met up with Calico Jack in jail, she said to him, *"I'm sorry to see you here, but if you'd have fought like a man you needn't hang like a dog."*

Mary Read

eanwhile, **Mary Read** had been roaming England disguised as a guy. She'd been raised as a boy by her mother who feared they'd lose their inheritance if Mary's grandmother knew she was a girl. At thirteen, Mom hired Mary out as a footboy. Later, Mary worked as a sailor, then a soldier, until she fell in love with another soldier and confessed her identity to him. The two got married and opened an inn, but there was to be no happily ever after. They were still in the honeymoon period when Mary's man died. Once again, Mary doffed her dresses and, disguised as a man, shipped off to the West Indies on a merchant vessel.

Her boat was captured by Anne and Calico Jack, and Mary was taken aboard their ship still in her disguise. Anne figured she'd take the young sailor as a prize for a piracy well done, but she soon found out that "he" was a "she." Mary assured her captor she'd rather join the pirates than lead the dull life of a woman, so Anne had her inaugurated as a member of the crew.

After their capture (see "When the Chips Are Down" sidebar), the remaining members were taken to prison and sentenced to hang. Anne and Mary admitted to being women and pleaded to be tried separately from the men. They claimed to be pregnant, knowing it was against the law to hang a woman carrying a child. It is uncertain whether they actually were pregnant, but they did succeed in having their executions delayed.

Some sources say that Mary died in jail after giving birth; accounts of Anne's fate vary in circumstance and plausibility. But who wants to imagine their landlocked endings anyway? Mary and Anne should be remembered doing what they loved best—stirring up trouble and courting adventure on the high seas.

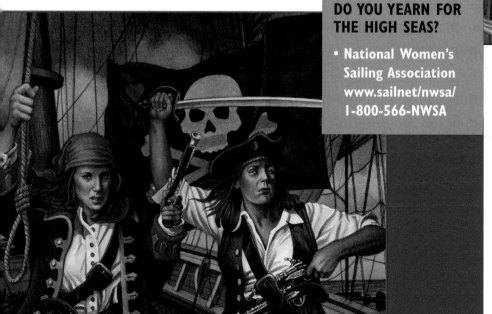

DO YOU YEARN FOR THE HIGH SEAS?

- **National Women's Sailing Association www.sailnet/nwsa/ 1-800-566-NWSA**

Romance, Pirate-Style

Legend has it that when a boyfriend of Mary Read's was threatened by another pirate and ultimately challenged to a duel, Mary couldn't stand to see her sweetheart in danger. She stepped in herself and killed the annoying challenger. Now *that's* true love.

Righteous Queens

WHO CAN RESIST ROYALTY?

Christina, Queen of Sweden

Let's face it—any woman who combines royal lineage with a renegade character is certain to be cool. Fact is, the history books are jam-packed with righteous lady leaders, making it nearly impossible to single out one or two. Think of these stories as a sampling of she-monarch magnificence—just a couple of the most righteous queens in history.

Christina was not one to chuck it all for a guy. In fact, you could say she chucked it all to avoid the guy. After reigning over Sweden from 1644 to 1654, Christina shocked Europe when, at the age of twenty-eight, she abdicated her throne.

Though she insisted she was ill, her aversion to marriage and her secret conversion to Catholicism were the driving forces behind her abdication: A queen was expected to marry and Christina wanted no part of it.

Whip-smart and politically shrewd from the start, Christina was educated as a prince and by the time she was fourteen was sitting in on council meetings. She'd become queen-elect before she was six, and at eighteen was officially crowned.

Often referred to as Minerva of the North (after the Greek goddess of wisdom), Christina rose at five each morning to read and she invited eminent foreign writers, musicians, and scholars to frequent her court. Also known for her extravagance, Christina cultivated a great collection of paintings, sculpture, and medallions and her enormous library of books and manuscripts is now on view in the Vatican.

Following her abdication, Christina was received by the Pope, but the headstrong woman upset him when she opposed his ideas about pious display. Regardless, Christina was well-received by the Roman people, but she missed being queen and began plotting to seize Naples from Spain. A born swashbuckler, Christina was willing to fight for the throne. But the scheme collapsed in 1657, as did much of Christina's support, when she ordered the execution of one of her officers, alleging his betrayal.

Of course the most famous accounting of Christina's life is the movie *Queen Christina* starring Greta Garbo.

Queen Christina © 1934 Turner Entertainment Co.

Eleanor of Aquitaine,
Queen of France and England

Just because she lived in the twelfth century, don't think Eleanor of Aquitaine wasn't a modern woman. Take her participation in the second crusade: When princes, dukes, and warriors set out on a military campaign to liberate the Holy Land, Eleanor donned her sexiest armor and rounded up her best girlfriends. Mounted on chargers with axes and spears at their sides, they scoured the country calling for volunteers to join the crusades.

Born to vast land holdings, Eleanor had cleverly combined her Aquitaine holdings (a province now part of France) with France's territory when she married Louis VII, who became King of France and made her Queen. When the two of them disagreed about the crusade route, Louis got his way, but Eleanor—by no means the demure, accepting wife—eventually got their marriage annulled and regained rule over the Aquitaine lands.

Not long after, Eleanor married a man ten years her junior—Henry II, who became King of England. But again Eleanor was underwhelmed by her choice in husband. Henry was a philanderer, not to mention a renowned glutton. At fifty, Eleanor expressed her resentment directly when she and two of her sons led the Aquitaine army against Henry's men. But the King prevailed and Eleanor spent the next fifteen years under house arrest. She regained her freedom when Henry died. Eleanor was still feeling spunky at eighty, and led her own army to defend her son's throne against rebel forces.

For a modern take on the decidedly stormy relationship between Henry and Eleanor (they were usually at war—literally), check out *The Lion in Winter* (1968), starring Peter O'Toole and Katharine Hepburn. Hepburn won an Oscar for her dead-on portrayal of fabulous Eleanor.

"If you've used an electric mixer in your kitchen, you can learn to run a drill press. If you've followed recipes exactly, you can learn to load shell."

—FROM A 1943 BILLBOARD AD

homemakers that traded in their baking pans and vacuum cleaners for blow torches and assembly lines. The U.S. government propaganda machine was hard at work, convincing women to enter the workplace and take over for their husbands, fathers, brothers, and boyfriends who were overseas fighting **the enemy.**

So, after decades of telling women that their sole duty was to stay home and take care of their children and keep a tidy home, there was a new message: **GET A JOB!**

If you've seen her image, you probably got the wrong impression. With her shirt sleeves rolled up and a defiant look on her face, **ROSIE THE RIVETER** looks like a militant when, in fact, she was just being the good girl Uncle Sam expected her to be.

"Rosie the Riveter" was a popular war propaganda symbol. Rosie was also a potent symbol for a generation of women: a patriotic description of the legions of

Thanks for nothing

After the war, the women pilots who had stepped in to fly planes while the men were away were offered airline jobs — as stewardesses.

(See separate profile on the W. A. S. P.s)

For most women, working outside the home was a new experience. Accustomed to the diligent work of keeping house, they made the transition beautifully. The defense industry alone hired two million female workers during the war. These maverick women quickly learned how to build huge airplanes and ships, put together machine guns, and wire electrical equipment. Altogether, six million women entered the labor force, including a large number of mothers and wives.

Quickly recognizing "Rosie's" value and abilities, the U.S. government reclassified women from a marginal to a basic labor resource. There were also serious racial barriers toppled, as black and white women worked side by side—perhaps for the first time in American history. While battles were being fought abroad, common ground was found here at home.

But I Like My Job!

Many of these women found working outside the home to be glamorous and rewarding. Some even planned to carry on a career after the war.

But after the fighting had ended, the machine that had so aggressively recruited women for jobs suddenly turned them away.

When Johnny came marching home, his job was waiting—and the women were sent home to don their aprons and bake brownies for the kids again. Some of the women didn't want to give up their newfound roles in the workplace, and fought to keep their jobs. Some were successful, but others who had worked diligently at heavy manual labor during the war were laughed out the door when they went looking for post-war work. Still, Rosie the Riveter's legacy was a new generation of women who knew they could make a living as well as any man. And did.

Rosie had started a revolution.

NOT ALL WOMEN WERE ROSIE
ABOUT 50,000 JAPANESE-AMERICAN
WOMEN SPENT THE WAR CONFINED
TO INTERNMENT CAMPS

It's Our Fight Too!

Lady Samurais

Long before the knights of Camelot, the Samurais set the standard for the noble warrior class. To make the grade as a samurai, you had to be strong, disciplined, and fearless, but you didn't necessarily have to be a man. Because in the war-torn lands that made up feudal Japan, every member of a samurai clan was expected to chip in to the defense of the tribe.

Just like the men, many of the women born into the prestigious samurai families of early Japan were trained in the basics of the fighting arts—handling the naginata sword, working the war horses, and generally learning the code of the most revered warrior class in history. Many of the women followed this training into full-fledged soldierhood, and a few earned a place as some of history's most celebrated samurais.

As early as the 600s A.D., there are records of fighting samurai women. The earliest account relates the story of a famous male samurai, Kamitsuken Katana, whose wife apparently grew tired of waiting home at the castle, and decided to pitch in to the fighting. (Typical of male-dominated historical texts, her name is not given.) Her renegade spirit apparently caught on, and she managed to recruit several more aspiring amazons. After some serious training in the finer points of weaponry—mostly with a bow and arrow—the samurai co-eds headed off to defend their land.

But for the most well-known female samurai, skip forward a few centuries to around 1200 A.D., when we find the story of legendary leader and warrior **Itagaki.** Her skills with the naginata sword and as a horsewoman earned her a spot as one of the most important leaders of the Taira clan of feudal Japan. Itagaki turned in many a valiant performance on the battlefield, but her most famous battle was her last. With her army hopelessly outnumbered by a margin of three to one, she refused to give up, instead calling on her men to defend their tribe to the end. She must have known that she had virtually no chance of survival, but according to historical accounts, Itagaki rode gallantly into the battle without a hint of surrender. She died like a true samurai warrior, with her sword drawn and her honor intact.

Dragon Ladies Supreme: Japan's History of Boss Women

According to the imperial chronology of Japan, its earlier years of monarchy were defined by women rulers. There were eight different women emperors before 770 A.D.

The Ballad of MuLan

Japan had no exclusive claim on righteous swordswomen. One of the world's most famed warrior women (albeit a fictional one) is MuLan—the subject of a celebrated Chinese poem written in the fourth or fifth century A.D.

In the poem, MuLan (which translates to "Magnolia") rides off to war in the place of her father and lives for years disguised as a man, leading a valiant soldier's life. She returns home triumphant, with none of her fellow soldiers discovering that she is a woman. When MuLan sheds her armor and appears in feminine dress, her countrymen are stunned that one of their greatest warriors is a woman.

ight around the same time, there were several other swordswomen making their mark on Japanese history.

One of the most famous was femme fighter *Hatsu-jo,* whose avenging exploits become part of Japanese legend through one of the country's most well-known kabuki plays. It wasn't that Hatsu-jo **looked** for trouble—just that some degenerate bad guy was always smearing her family name, forcing her to kick booty in true avenging tradition. This *Dirty Harry* scenario seemed to follow her everywhere, and she had to kill at least one deserving miscreant who had mistreated her loved ones.

There were a few other famous female avengers whose paths you just didn't want to cross: History books also record the wrath of swordswoman *Miyagino,* who hunted down the murderer of her father, and who was motivated by the same kind of avenging code. Or consider the story of famed swordswoman *Tora Gozen,* who helped out two revenge-seeking brothers in search of justice.

Although the vigilantism of these fighting women might seem a bit bloodthirsty by today's standards, this kind of justice was just about all there was to keep people in line before dialing "911" was an option.

In fact, self-preservation was the rule of the day. The doctrine of **kataki-uchi**—kind of an honorable code of revenge—was all the rage in feudal Japan, making vigilantism a sanctioned code of conduct. Avenging themes also played well on stage, making the story of the hero forced to take matters into her own hands a favorite of dramatists.

Margaret Sanger

The Rebel with a Cause

*Some called her the Savior of the Poor, or our Lady of Contraception. In any case, count **Margaret Sanger** as one of the bravest women of the twentieth century for taking on a forbidden issue—birth control. A nurturer at heart, her passion was ignited by the terrible suffering she witnessed in the poorest neighborhoods of New York City. Sanger simply saw too many women die before their time, and decided one day that something must be done.*

Margaret Sanger's baptism into the real plight of American women transformed her from an ordinary public health nurse to a radical rabble-rouser for the poor. Her dream was simple—that poor women would someday have the same access to birth control as the well-to-do. With this revolutionary idea, she became the leader of the twentieth-century campaign for reproductive rights, and thus changed the lives of millions of women forever.

An Unlikely Rebel
Etched in history as a militant Mother Teresa, Margaret Sanger's quiet life as a nurse and homemaker changed dramatically when she and her family moved to New York City in 1910.

As a visiting nurse in the slums that made up New York's Lower East Side shortly after the turn of the century, Margaret's interest in a woman's right to choose when—and if—she was ready to have a child stemmed from her work with the poor. These women, who struggled to put food on the table, had no access to or understanding of contraception. In families where there were just two or three babies—another came, and yet another. Women grew old before their time because of the strain of multiple pregnancies, and gave birth to children they could not feed. This phenomenon contributed greatly to the number of poor children on the streets who had to beg to survive.

Margaret decided to do something about it, and began dispensing much-needed advice about birth control. Poor women began to look to her as their savior, and she soon became a sage of the slums.

The Woman Rebel
In 1914 she founded the magazine *Woman Rebel*, which spoke frankly about the body and reproduction. For this seemingly innocent action, Margaret was indicted on obscenity charges.

Margaret's mother had died at the age of forty-seven after having eleven children and seven miscarriages.

"All children should be wanted and loved. That's the goal of everything I do."

Margaret's Legacy Lives On
Margaret Sanger
CENTER INTERNATIONAL
26 Bleecker Street, New York City

not to have any more children than their health could stand or their husbands support." For this outlandish behavior, she was arrested and dragged off to jail for thirty days. Her lawyers filed an appeal that not only freed her from jail, but won a landmark decision making it possible for doctors to give their patients information about birth control.

The indictment was dropped, but the incident fueled Sanger's indignance toward the institutions that controlled women's bodies.

In 1916, in the Brownsville section of Brooklyn, Margaret founded the first birth control clinic—ever. She and associates handed out leaflets in Yiddish, Italian, and English to advertise the landmark clinic's opening. As Margaret put it, "Women . . . flocked to the clinic with the determination

This was the beginning of a new world for women. To truly understand the importance of this decision, consider this: between 1910 and 1915, 300,000 women died in childbirth. That's more than all the men who died in U.S. wars from the Revolution to World War I.

But Margaret knew the war was not won, as women were still seriously limited in their access to birth control, and she kept up her fight. Finally, after World War II and decades of

contempt, ridicule, and arrest, the government became concerned about the exploding population and decided that she had a point. In 1936, the courts finally allowed doctors to legally prescribe birth control to women who wanted it. Margaret had won her fight, and women had her to thank for the right to control the growth of their own families. And that's why women everywhere, to this day, think of Margaret Sanger as a saint.

Sanger herself coined the term "birth control" in 1914.

Dear Mrs. Sanger: May 20, 1921

I would like to ask you to help me as soon as you can. I am a mother of 11 children, 10 living. Green, that is what I am, only 34 years old and am 3 months in a family way again. I have a man that thinks it's my fault because we have children. I do confess it is. I am out here on the farm, no money or way to get to the doctors. I would now take poison, for I do hate life again. Our children are all very strong and healthy, but I am the one who has to suffer. Can you not tell me or help me in some way? I have a daughter 17 and 15. I want them to know and be better than I, for this is sure hell.

Mrs. S.J., Minnesota

81

Soldaderas
Mexican Revolutionaries

When the people of Mexico rose up in revolt against the ruling classes, women everywhere joined the fight. But while men like Pancho Villa and Emiliano Zapata became heroes, the female leaders who fought so valiantly at their side were nearly lost in the history books. Here, to set the record straight, are a few of the coolest heroines in Mexican history—*the fighting Soldaderas.*

Many of the fighting soldaderas adopted dashing male pseudonyms like La Coronela, La Chata, and La Corredora.

Fighting the Good Fight—

The Mexican Revolution of 1910 was one of the most dramatic events of the twentieth century. The people came from everywhere to join the grassroots effort— peasants came from the mountains, workers from the villages, and intellectuals from the schools— all to fight for their beliefs. And among these rebels were a number of women leading the way. These female freedom fighters were everywhere—battling at the front lines, making speeches from the podiums, and writing the manifestos that would lead to a new future.

Dolores Jimenez y Muro was the kind of rebel that dictators hate—outspoken, fearless, and willing to risk everything for the sake of her country. She became one of the greatest leaders of the Revolution, stirring the Mexican people with her impassioned words and brilliant political critiques.

Dolores became a respected and popular figure within the movement, but paid the price for her prominence. She was arrested, threatened, and thrown in jail for her work. As her fame and influence grew, the government identified her as one of the most dangerous leaders in the country, and targeted her for frequent harassment. In fact, Dolores was so prominent in the movement that when the famous rebel leader Emiliano Zapata began to organize his armies, he named her a brigadier general. In 1917, when the new constitution was created, Dolores was one of the key contributors to its framework.

Or consider the rousing example of **Juana Belen Gutierrez de Mendoza,** a natural successor to Dolores as Government Enemy #1. (She was born about thirty years later.) As a champion of the people, she became one of the most outspoken voices of the revolutionary movement. Juana started her career as a rebel at a young age, inspired by the story of her grandfather who died for his political beliefs in front of a firing squad.

As an adult, she put her indignity to work, throwing all of her energy behind the revolution. She started a newspaper, *Vesper,* which became a central voice for the rebels and a powerful critic of the social order. Her writings posed enough of a threat to the government to get her printing presses confiscated, land her in jail, and eventually get her thrown out of the country.

Juana also took to the battlefield for her beliefs, and served with the Zapatista armies, where she was given the rank of colonel. She continued to struggle as an agent of change well past her youthful years. At the age of sixty, she published a newspaper called *Alma Mexicana,* and told an interviewer that she would not retire, saying that *"in all the world's corners lives a pain; . . . and I don't have the indifference to ignore it, nor the cowardice to flee it . . ."*

In fact, both Juana and Dolores continued to work for their beliefs until the end of their lives. Though they were always looking ahead to new battles, they surely must have realized the impact they made on the fate of their country, and on the fortunes of their people—forever.

Once a rebel always a rebel

Dolores didn't slow down in her later years, and had the distinction of having a price put on her head by the government when she was nearly seventy years old.

The Bravest Caretaker

One of the most famous Soldaderas, **Beatriz Gonzalez Ortega** was better known for healing than fighting. She was a tireless nurse on the battlefield, and often helped the wounded from both sides. She even defied the great Pancho Villa after one battle, refusing to tell him which of her patients were from the other side, since she knew that they would be executed. She had hidden their uniforms, and even when she was whipped, she refused to identify the luckless men. She eventually earned the respect of Villa for her bravery.

"When many men have lost heart and, out of cowardice, retired from the fight . . . there are brave women, ready to fight for our principles."

—another Mexican paper on the efforts and writing of Juana Gutierrez de Mendoza

Soviet Flying Aces of WWII

Legends of Soviet history, the female fighter pilots who served during World War II were some of the most heroic aviators to ever do battle. The female aces proved once and for all that a woman could be as formidable when defending her country as any man. At first, the Germans laughed at the female pilots, but they soon came to respect, and ultimately fear the women they would nickname **the Night Witches of the Skies**.

During World War II, the Soviet Union called upon a number of Russian women to help in the aerial defense of the country from invading German armies. The women were expected to stick to "easy" duties like transporting equipment, but the squadrons of female pilots turned out to be some of the most heroic and skilled fighters in the country's arsenal.

Lily Litvak was the most legendary of the squadron pilots, destroying twelve German fighter planes during her short time in combat. She was easily recognized in the skies by the white rose painted on her plane. Lily's dogfighting skills were famous—she was particularly well known for her loop maneuver: With the enemy on her tail, Lily would suddenly pull straight up and backwards until she was upside down, and then swoop in behind the other plane

for the dominant combat position. As her fame grew, so did the determination of her enemies—every German pilot wanted to be the one to kill the famous "girl pilot" with the white rose. Lily was finally downed in a spectacular aerial battle in which she was wildly outnumbered. Other pilots who witnessed her last battle say it took eight German planes to take down the greatest lady pilot ever, Lily Litvak.

Lily was known by the white rose painted on her plane.

More on the Soviet Flying Aces:

▲ *NIGHT WITCHES*
Bruce Myles, Presidio Press

▲ *A DANCE WITH DEATH: SOVIET AIR WOMEN OF WORLD WAR II*
Anne Noggle, Texas A&M Press

Lily Litvak   Katerina Fedotova   Vera Tarasova

ONE OF THE MOST FAMOUS STORIES of the Soviet aces tells of the day that two of the woman pilots took on forty-two (that's right 4-2) German fighter planes in a dogfight that has now become Russian military legend. When the two women, out on a routine sortie, came across a formation of German planes flying below, they knew they had no choice. They had clearly stumbled upon a massive enemy bombing run that would have to be stopped at all costs. They dived on the enemy planes in a virtual suicide attack. They managed to destroy three of the German planes, and—more importantly—forced the planes to abandon their mission. Miraculously, both Soviet aces survived—one parachuted out of her burning plane after it was hit, and the other managed a crash landing.

Russian farmers and peasants who greeted them on the ground were amazed when they realized that the two daring pilots were women. The incredible story of the two lady flyers who had taken on an army of German planes was carried all over the world.

OR CONSIDER THE STORY OF **Ira Kasherina's** bravest day. Imagine being the navigator of a crippled plane flying through enemy fire. Then imagine that your pilot—and friend—has been killed in the cockpit. Now you've got a glimpse of Ira's worst wartime experience. Even more terrible, when she tried to take over the duplicate controls in the back of the plane, she realized that her friend's lifeless body—slumped over the controls—was keeping the aircraft from responding. Ira had to stand up and fly through enemy fire while stretched across to the other cockpit so she could hold her friend's corpse off of the controls. Later, when she was asked why she didn't dump the body out of the plane to make things easier, she said that would have been an unthinkable thing to do to her friend.

Fighting the Fear

None of the SOVIET FLYING ACES would remember their wartime experience as glamorous. Many of their outings ended with a count of who among them had been killed, and the fight to overcome the stomach-churning fear that came with their duties was never-ending. One pilot, OLGA YEMSHOKOVA, learned to build time into her take-off routine to throw up.

The planes used by the Soviet pilots were not as advanced as those of the Germans. Most of the steering was done with a **throttle** in front of the pilot, along with **rudder pedals** on the floor. Because the Soviet planes were at an advantage closer to the ground, a pilot's first reaction to a sudden attack was usually to push down with all her might into a dive.

The firing button was on the **control stick,** and would control all three of the guns mounted on the plane. To release a **bomb,** which was simply attached to the bottom of the wings, the pilot would pull a wire inside the cockpit. The navigation tools were archaic compared to today—the women used **stopwatches** and maps to find their way through the skies.

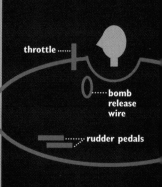

throttle ......

...... bomb release wire

...... rudder pedals

Lady Spies

Nerves of steel, a taste for danger, and a passion to make a difference— it takes a special kind of person to be a secret agent. But time and time again, women have answered the call of espionage, and become some of the world's most legendary spies. In fact, being female could be the most effective weapon in an agent's arsenal. Who would suspect that behind the guise of a harried housewife or a beautiful siren could be the most treacherous of undercover threats—the mysterious and captivating

Lady Spy?

And in the history of espionage, no story is more thrilling than that of *Amy Thorpe Pack*—the ultimate femme fatale of spydom.

Hers was a deadly combination—beauty, brains, and a cool head under pressure. She learned early on that men were easy prey for her charms, and used them ruthlessly to gain secrets for Britain during World War II. Her career included many triumphs, but her greatest achievements occurred during her time in Washington D.C.

Amy targeted the Vichy French embassy, with the specific objective of stealing their military code. (The Vichy French were sided against the Allies.) She and her contact made a daring plan. They would break into the embassy, let in a safe cracker through a window, then pass the codebooks out to be photographed and replaced before dawn. It was a harrowing night, and Amy had to think fast on her feet, but when morning came, their mission was accomplished. Amy delivered the code to the British without the French embassy ever knowing it had been stolen. It turned out to be one of the most valuable advantages in the Allied arsenal during WWII, and Pack's supervisor would say later that she was responsible for saving 100,000 Allied lives.

On the night that Mrs. Pack stole the code from the French Embassy, there was only one snag. A security guard grew suspicious and tried to come into the room where they were working. Amy convinced him that she was having a tryst with her boyfriend, and he quickly left, embarrassed.

The Myth of Mata Hari

Probably the most famous of female spies is the legendary Mata Hari—born Margareth Zelle. Although her life as an exotic dancer (with a fabricated past) was terribly exciting, Mata Hari was actually a pretty terrible spy. She switched sides often, and was unsuccessful at obtaining information for anybody. When she was executed by a French firing squad for being a German informer, the resulting sensation made her story world-famous.

BREAKING THE CODE

One of the most important things that a spy could acquire was another country's secret code—sometimes called a cipher—which was used to scramble their military communications.

But the other side had plenty of ace female agents, too.

Take, for example, *Ruth Kuczynski Beurton*— one of the most brilliant Soviet agents of her day. Based in Britain during most of her career, her success lay in her ability to appear completely ordinary— how could this frumpy "hausfrau" be a sinister communist threat? From her unassuming little cottage, she used a short-wave radio to transmit information to her country. Only after she had escaped back to her country, did British agents realize the enormity of the hausfrau's operation—she had been the head of the famous operation SONIA—the most damaging Soviet espionage ring to occupy Britain during WWII.

Beurton often transported undercover materials inside her son's teddy bear. No one would suspect a mother traveling with her little boy, his teddy bear in hand.

Secret Agents and the Civil War

Harriet Tubman was the most famous Civil War lady spy, (see her separate profile) but there were plenty of other capable women working undercover.

"Crazy Bet" (Elizabeth Van Lew) used a convincing act as a deranged woman to find out all she could for the Union side. She smuggled messages inside hollowed-out eggs to Union soldiers, muttering to herself as she walked along with her innocent vegetable baskets.

On the other side of the conflict, **Belle Boyd** was one of the Confederacy's finest agents. She personally carried messages to the front lines, dodging bullets when she had to, and ending up in jail many times for her efforts. She was fiercely loyal to the cause of the Rebels, and once shot a soldier who tried to raise the Union flag over her house.

Belle Boyd

The Suffragists

Don't let the skirts fool you— the Suffragists were the toughest group of rabble-rousing rebels ever to wreak havoc on a system stuck in the past. Along the way they were spit on, beaten up, and ridiculed by all sides. But these women were on fire for something they knew we all deserved—they were fighting for YOU, and YOUR right to vote.

"We are women, American women

That's right—not so long ago women weren't considered human enough to qualify as full citizens. Pretty incredible, huh? In fact, it was less than eighty years ago that American women cast their first vote. For most of our nation's history, women have had no say in the government or how it was run. That was when the fighting suffragists hit the scene.

These women weren't about to take no for an answer. In the United States, and other countries worldwide, these troublemakers didn't just stir things up, they started a movement that spanned nearly a century, and divided more than one country.

It was an all-out war—and don't let anyone tell you otherwise. Women fought, and died, for the right to have a simple say in the way their country was run. Because many suffragists were also fighting for abolition— the movement to free the slaves—they were reviled within their towns, churches, and social circles. On the streets they were treated like common criminals: ridiculed, arrested, and even murdered. But they didn't give up. These women knew they were right, and they didn't stop fighting until they won.

It was a long, messy, and exhausting fight, spanning generations of fighting women. But in 1920, the Nineteenth Amendment to the United States Constitution was ratified, guaranteeing that no state could deny the right to vote on the basis of sex.

SO when YOU get the chance to vote, USE IT

AND don't forget to say a little THANK YOU to the

SISTERS WHO GAVE IT TO YOU.

"I look upon myself as a prisoner of war."
—British suffragist leader
EMMELINE PANKHURST
after being arrested outside
Buckingham Palace

A WOMAN'S FURY . . .

After trying to get things done the "lady-like" way, suffragists knew their tactics had to become more extreme if women were ever to win the right to vote.

Suffragists broke windows, started fires, and wrote "Votes for Women" in acid on golf courses. They were regularly attacked by angry mobs, and usually arrested.

In the ultimate act of martyrdom, English suffragist Emily Davison went to the Epson Derby in 1913 and threw herself in front of a horse. She died of her injuries, and the furor over the incident reignited a firestorm of attention for the struggle to win the vote.

Got politics in your blood?

Get in touch with these groups in Washington for more info:

Rock the Vote
www.rockthevote.org

League of Women Voters
www.lwv.org
1730 M Street, NW
Washington, DC 20036-4508
(202) 429-1965

THE REBEL LEADERS

Susan B. Anthony ➤
& Elizabeth Cady Stanton

Suffragist Tactics: The Hunger Strike

One of the most effective tools used by the suffragists was the hunger strike—once arrested, the women would refuse to eat. The prospect of women dying in jail was hugely embarrassing to the government, and did much to raise public sympathy for the cause.

*C*redit these maverick women for changing your life. The two women who laid the groundwork for our freedom to vote never got a chance to voice their choice. Already activists for women's rights, Anthony and Stanton attended the landmark women's rights convention at Seneca Falls, New York in 1848 and started a movement that would long outlive them.

Susan B. Anthony quickly emerged as the leader of the American women's rights movement and along with Stanton, her lifetime pal, formally introduced the American Suffrage Amendment to the Constitution in 1878. Informally called the Anthony Amendment, it was first voted on and shot down in 1886. Anthony and Stanton weren't around to cast the first ballots, but they trained an army of suffragists who saw their work through to its constitutional finish.

Harriet Tubman

FIERCE FREEDOM FIGHTER

Adventurer, warrior, master spy—

You name the dangerous calling, and Harriet took it on. During her lifetime, Harriet Tubman developed into one of the most effective and daring rebels in American history. Harriet's courage was fueled by her resentment at the system into which she had been born—slavery.

Harriet just wasn't the type to accept the status quo. After thinking long and hard about the way things were and the way things should be, Harriet took action. At the age of twenty-nine, she began her career as slavery's worst nightmare when she escaped to freedom in the North. Still not satisfied, she went back for her sister and children the next year, and eventually her brothers and mother. Harriet had found her calling, and the fierce "Black Moses" was born. During her work as a getaway expert, she helped hundreds of people escape from the tyranny of slavery on nearly twenty perilous missions into the South. Her trips became all the more dangerous as her notoriety grew. Slave owners were desperate to capture her, and offered the huge sum of $40,000 for her arrest.

Harriet was referred to as the "Black Moses" because of her skill at leading her people to freedom. Of course, others simply called her "Genera

Harriet's success was attributed to her meticulous planning and clever plots—she was a master at planning the details of her trips. She outsmarted her would-be captors by purchasing unused train tickets, and carried sedatives for babies who might cry and give them away. She was also a fierce disciplinarian, reportedly using a revolver to change the mind of anyone who got cold feet and wanted to turn back.

Harriet's life of adventure continued during the Civil War, when she served as a soldier and undercover spy for the North. At one point she was in command of several river gunboats, which destroyed key Southern targets and freed hundreds of slaves. In her work as an undercover agent, Harriet crossed enemy lines in the South to gather important intelligence, often from slaves.

Despite her recognized contributions to the Union Army during the Civil War—all Union officers were obliged to tip their hat when passing her—Harriet was not rewarded with a soldier's pension until thirty years after the fighting ended.

After the war, Harriet's interest in righting wrongs was just as strong, and she continued to work hard to help the causes she cared about, raising money for schools, helping former slaves, and working for the sick and destitute. She established the Harriet Tubman Home for the Aged and Indigent Colored People, where she herself lived in old age until she died in 1913. The cause of freedom will never be the same.

The price on Harriet's head was an enormous $40,000—reflecting the desperation of the slave owners who wanted her captured and the threat she represented to their system.

Viking Women

Erik the Red, Leif Erikson—everybody knows the names of the most famous Viking men, all big and bearded, plundering their way across the globe in their great Viking ships. The popular Viking image is a decidedly manly one, and to judge from most sources, one would think that women were nowhere to be found. Wrong again, of course. The sagas of Scandinavia's greatest adventurers are filled with the stories of women who loved a good adventure as much as their male counterparts—these are some of the greatest Viking Women.

The Viking age is roughly defined as the period 800 to 1100 A.D., but the historical records of the Vikings are a cryptic mix of fact and fiction. The famous Viking "sagas" (long, poetic narratives written by pseudo-historians and dramatists) are thought to be based on real events and characters, but with heavy doses of poetic license to make for a better story. Still, even if the narratives are not entirely factual, they are generally acknowledged as a reliable sign of the times. And judging from the best sagas, there were plenty of Viking women bossing their way around the Scandinavian seas.

Take, for example, the slightly unsettling tales of the Red Maiden, which pop up in the narratives of ancient Irish texts. The stories are a bit sketchy—as with many Viking narratives—but apparently Old Red had the Irish shaking in their boots. According to her sagas, she was the leader of the most brutal attacks on Ireland during the tenth century, which doesn't make her much of a role model, but certainly qualifies her as a bonified Viking. Did she really exist? As with so many characters in the sagas—we can never be sure.

Probably the most famous of Viking strong-women are the legendary Valkyries—the mythological overseers of the sacred Valhall. In Norse mythology, Valhall is the place where all slain warriors go to relax after the trauma of battle and the stress of, well, getting killed. It's a cheery sort of underworld, and the Valkyries are there to generally supervise the proceedings. But more important is their power to decide who gets in—according to legend, it is the Valkyries who go to the battlefield and decide which warriors will live or die.

Or for more active Viking women, you might turn to the scribblings of a certain Saxo Grammaticus—a man clearly obsessed with the notion of Viking amazons. His *History of Danes*, written around 1200 A.D., is thought to be partly based on truth, but, as always, with plenty of fantasy thrown in for entertainment value.

Through Saxo's writings, we learn the story of Rusila, a power-hungry leader who fought her brother ferociously for the throne of Norway, winning battle after battle, until she was finally defeated. Saxo also writes of women warriors at the great Norse battle of Brávellir: Hetha and Visna, *"whose female bodies nature had endowed with manly courage,"* and Vebiorg, who *"instilled with the same spirit, led companies of men on the Danish side."* In the story, Visna and Vebiorg are killed in the battle, but Hetha survives to become a ruler of Denmark.

Real women? Who knows? But many historians believe that the forcefulness of even these fictional characters points to real-life Viking women who must have been pretty powerful prototypes.

Probably the most widely recognized image of the Viking woman is of the opera singer with the horns on her head. While it makes for an appealing picture, truth is, this particular accessory just wasn't in the Viking wardrobe.

It's All in the Packaging

Ever wonder how the arctic country of Greenland got its name? According to the saga of Erik the Red, he sneakily gave it that name so it would be more attractive to new settlers. Let's face it—who'd want to move to Icebergland?

"The Valkyrie"
oil painting by John Gruse

Sons and Datters

Chances are if you meet a girl from Iceland, her last name will end with "datter." That's because Icelanders still use the Old Norse naming system. If you're the daughter of Jon, your last name would be "Jonsdatter" (i.e., Jon's daughter) and your brother's last name would be "Jonson." This makes for a confusing number of Jonsdatters, as you can imagine, which is why everybody goes by their first name—even in the phone book.

Aud the Explorer

For a lady Viking more based in fact, look to Aud the Deep-Minded—a saga-subject widely agreed to have been a real woman. (Who could make up a name like that?)

As related in the Icelandic saga of Laxdoela, Aud's story is one of wanderlust, and she comes across as one of the most powerful Viking explorers.

Her journey began when she became so annoyed with the King of Norway that she decided to pack up and move to a better continent. Aud was evidently a woman in charge, because soon enough she'd moved the whole family, lock, stock and barrel, across the seas to Scotland. She and her clan settled there for a while, but after her father and son died, she decided that life would be easier in Iceland.

Upon reaching the new land, Aud sailed around the continent claiming any land that struck her fancy, and granting it to her various offspring and followers. Her last act was to throw a great wedding party for her grandson, and, after telling her guests to enjoy themselves, she promptly went upstairs to die. Always the gracious monarch, Aud just didn't want to spoil the party.

Madame C. J. Walker

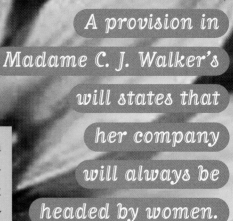

The fact is that Sarah Breedlove became the first black woman millionaire in the United States because of a bad hair day. The year was 1905, Sarah lived in St. Louis, Missouri, and by bad hair day, we don't mean the frizzies. Sarah's hair was falling out and she prayed to God to save it. But Sarah clearly wasn't one to twiddle her thumbs waiting for divine intervention. Her hairy situation gave her the idea to start a company featuring hair care products. Sarah said the formula for the first product she created—for hair growth—came to her in a dream.

A provision in Madame C. J. Walker's will states that her company will always be headed by women.

Next, she invented a new system for straightening black hair which included a hair softener and a special metal heating comb. Many people accused Sarah of trying to make black women look more white—but she strenuously denied this. Her goal was to "Beautify Black America" by creating hair products that did not harm "African-American hair."

Before she began selling her products, Sarah, showing her finesse for marketing, added the "Madame" to her name so people would know she was married (to Charles J. Walker) and to give her products an extra cachet. Voilà, Madame C. J. Walker was born and she boldly hit the streets, taking her inventions door-to-door.

Madame C. J.'s hard work paid off big-time—five years later, she was rich enough to build the Madame C. J. Walker Manufacturing Company in Indianapolis, Indiana, where she employed three thousand people. Clearly, women loved her product. When it came to straightening, the alternative for black women at that time was to lay their hair on a flat surface and press it with an iron. *Can you smell burnt hair?* Madame Walker's fame spread to Europe when word got out that Paris' darling, Josephine Baker (see her separate profile) had the Walker System to thank for her "do."

As sole owner and president of the company, Madame Walker managed an expanding empire which included her factory, the Walker College of Hair Culture, a mail-order business, and droves of Walker agents who demonstrated and sold the beauty line in neighborhoods throughout the United States. She was proud to be a black entrepreneur and made a point of hiring black employees.

What's a Walker Agent?

Before Avon ladies, there were Walker agents. One of Madame Walker's proudest achievements was the number of women she employed, and the agents became familiar figures in the United States and the Caribbean where they made "house calls." They hit the streets wearing white shirtwaists tucked into long black skirts, and carrying black bags full of Walker beauty products.

All agents were required to sign contracts specifying the exclusive use of C. J. Walker products and methods, but also binding them to a hygienic regimen. Madame Walker visited her agents frequently and preached "cleanliness and loveliness" as assets and aids to self-respect and racial advancement.

Madame Walker divided her agents into Walker Clubs and encouraged them to support black philanthropic work. At the yearly convention of Walker agents, she always gave cash prizes to the local affiliate that had done the most community work.

Before Madame Walker died, there were more than two thousand agents demonstrating the Walker System for treating hair and selling the ever-expanding line of Walker products.

But You Don't Know the Half of It...

Not only was Madame C. J. Walker a marketing genius and one of the most successful executives of the early twentieth century, but she accomplished her fame and fortune against all odds. She was born in Delta, Louisiana, on December 23, 1867, orphaned at five, married by fourteen, then widowed at age twenty when her husband was lynched. She moved to St. Louis and supported herself and her daughter A'Lelia for eighteen years as a washerwoman. That's when Sarah turned a bad hair day into big bucks, and said bye-bye to washing other people's dirty laundry.

Madame Walker died in her villa at the age of fifty-one. Against doctor's orders, she had continued her busy schedule until kidney failure and hypertension got the best of her. After her mother's death, her daughter A'Lelia followed in her mom's headline-making footsteps, hosting a gathering known as "The Dark Tower." The guest list included talented black musicians, artists, and authors and influential white intellectuals, publishers, critics, and patrons. (See separate profile on the Harlem Renaissance.)

the fearless flying W.A.S.Ps

"We are Yankee Doodle pilots,
Yankee Doodle, do or die.
Real live nieces of our Uncle Sam,
Born with a yearning to fly . . .

During World War II, one of the most striking experiments in military history fell smack dab into the middle of a small town in West Texas. There, thousands of women from around the country reported to the first all-female pilot training base in the world. They called them the **WOMEN AIR FORCE SERVICE PILOTS,** better known by the most dashing new handle in the military— the WASPs.

But don't give the U.S. Army credit for the concept— they were dead-set against the notion of female flyers. The WASPs were the brainchild of Jackie Cochran—one of the most famous women pilots during the 1930s and 1940s. Cochran knew that the allied war effort needed pilots, and that the thousands of American women licensed to fly were the obvious solution to the shortfall. But the military was stuck in the men-only mindset that defined the times, and refused to believe that women had what it took to serve in the air.

After lobbying for two years, Jackie gave up on the Army and created a program to help out

Madge Leon Moore, Margaret Chamberlain Tamplin, Alyce Stevens Rohrer

the British allies in ferrying aircraft. That program, which used only women pilots, was a resounding success, and suddenly the U.S. government was interested in Cochran's idea. With the Army's blessing, she put out a call for female pilots to train on military aircraft. She had about 2,000 spots to fill, and there was some skepticism about whether she would find enough women willing to take on such dangerous work. The response was stunning—25,000 women clamored to join Cochran's troops.

Secretaries, homemakers, and teachers from all over the country sent in applications, eager to serve their country and find adventure in the wild blue yonder.

The training was comprehensive and grueling. Graduates were expected to master all tricky aerial maneuvers like loops and spins. Aside from their standard ferrying duties (usually delivering planes from the factory to the domestic takeoff point), the WASPs tested defective planes, put new planes through dangerous maneuvers, and dragged targets for male fighter pilots in training.

The WASPs learned to fly every type of plane used by the military, from the fastest pursuit planes (like the P-47 "Thunderbolt"), and the heavy-duty bombers (like the B-17 "Flying Fortress"). Only the most talented pilots passed the program—of the original 1,830 women accepted for training, only 1,074 made the grade.

Short-lived as it was, the WASP program proved once and for all that women were just as suited to fly for the military as men. In the final report about the program, Cochran noted that women demonstrated the same endurance as men, learned just as quickly, and had similar safety records.

Although WASPs completed the same rigorous training as male pilots, and devoted years of their lives to the WASP program, the U.S. government refused to grant them military status. This meant that they had no military benefits (insurance, for example—something you might want in that line of work), they had to pay their own way to the training site, and were required to supply their own clothes at the beginning of the program.

Any pilot who managed to bail out of her plane and survive was considered an official member of the "Caterpillar Club." One WASP joined the club when her safety belt snapped open during a spin and she fell out. They found her later walking back to base, clutching her official club entry requirement— the ripcord handle from her parachute.

Margaret Chamberlain Tamplin, Madge Leon Moore, Alyce Stevens Rohrer

When a WASP died in action, as thirty-eight of them did, the U.S. Army would not cover the costs of the funeral, or even pay for transporting the body home.

As the war neared a close, the WASPs disbanded at the end of 1944 after only two years in operation. The women who had sacrificed, worked, and even died for their country were not given the thanks of military recognition, nor benefits. In 1977, after more than thirty years of being slighted by their own country, President Jimmy Carter signed a bill conferring official military status on the WASPs.

Dorothy Britt Mann

Jackie Cochran's record alone should have been enough to clue the Army into sky-high girl power. She was the first woman to fly faster than the speed of sound, and still holds more aviation records than any other pilot in history— man or woman.

Do YOU have a yen for the Wild Blue Yonder? Try these sites for info:

- THE NINETY-NINES—Organization of female pilots
  www.ninety-nines.org • (800) 994-1929

- YOUNG EAGLES PROGRAM—Flying group for kids and teens
  P.O. Box 2683 • Oshkosh, WI 54903 • (414) 426-4831 • www.eaa.org

Mae West

Mae West blew into Hollywood like a one-woman tornado of feminine strength. She shocked, scandalized, and shimmied her way into the hearts of an adoring public, and pushed aside the prudish warnings of studio bosses and censors. Offstage, she was one of the most powerful businesswomen during a time when most actors had virtually no control over their careers. In all aspects of her life, Mae West's approach was simple and direct—she saw what she wanted, and simply took it.

Mae's legacy lives on in plenty of movies—check out the classics:

- *My Little Chickadee*
- *I'm No Angel*
- *Klondike Annie*

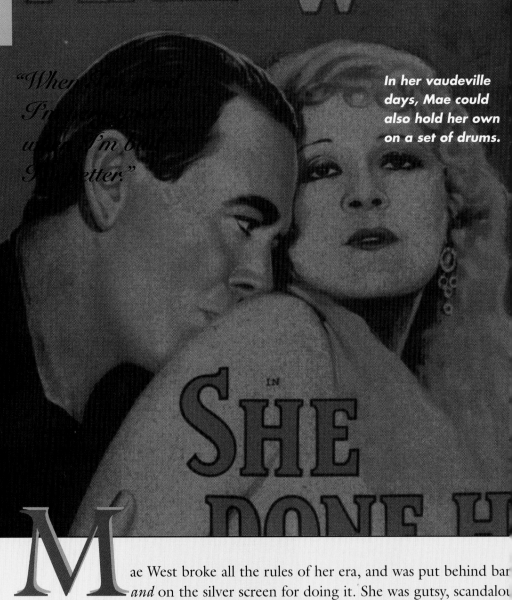

"When ... I'm ... when I'm b... the better."

In her vaudeville days, Mae could also hold her own on a set of drums.

Mae West broke all the rules of her era, and was put behind bars *and* on the silver screen for doing it. She was gutsy, scandalous and for the most part, followed this advice from her mom: Never let a man jeopardize your rise to stardom by marrying you into a life of domestic drudgery. Of course she certainly had nothing against men—in fact, she married one when she was just seventeen years old. Unfortunately, she regretted the marriage immediately and she and her husband separated. Mae: ***"Marriage is a great institution . . . but I'm not ready for an institution."***

Trademark wisecracks like that became as big a part of her persona as her famous hourglass figure.

The Bombshell with a Head for Business

Beneath the wisecracking was a brainy femme fatale. Mae West did everything from write and produce plays to act, sing, dance, and perform comedy. She controlled her career by picking her parts and writing her own lines—which was unprecedented at the time. She even chose leading man Cary Grant by saying, "If he can talk, I'll take him."

From Shimmy to Slammer

While World War I shook up the world, Mae did some shaking of her own with a Jazz Age dance called The Shimmy. There was some disagreement over who really invented it, to which Mae responded: "Who wants to make a career of the shakes anyway?" Clearly, not Mae. She followed the shimmy with some notoriety when she wrote and starred in a controversial play she called Sex. Remember this was 1925, and her play was considered scandalous beyond belief. The show closed when the police raided it, arresting the cast, producers, and directors on corruption charges. Mae fought the charges; she took center court at the trial and reportedly gave a stellar performance, playing heavily to the gallery. When the judge warned her of contempt, she shot back, "I'm doing my best to hide it, Your Honor."

Unfortunately, Mae needed more than a good performance to avoid jail time.

That experience didn't stop Mae from writing another box-office smash—a play called Diamond Lil. It was a huge hit, and her next stop was Hollywood.

Mae started her Hollywood career with a tiny scene in the movie Night After Night (see "The Scene That Made Her a Star" below), but it was enough. Movie audiences everywhere loved it, and a star was born.

More Blonde Ambition

Mae went on to make several more blockbusters, and for a time she was the highest paid actress in Hollywood. Although she was one of the most popular stars of the screen, she was constantly scrutinized by groups like The Legion of Decency and the Hayes Committee, who edited and censored her screenplays. Mae died in 1980 when she was eighty-seven years old. The woman lived fast and long or—as she once said, **"I've been things and I've seen places."**

The Scene That Made Her a Star

Mae saunters in to a nightclub, strikes a pose—hand on hip and dripping diamonds. HAT CHECK GIRL: "Goodness, what lovely diamonds."

MAE: "Goodness had nothing to do with it, dearie."

Born on August 17, 1892, in Brooklyn, Mae was bringing down the house by the time she was eight. Her gig: song and dance numbers and impersonations at afternoon amateur vaudeville shows. As a teenager, she learned to play the drums and worked percussion into her shows.

THE BRAINS BENEATH ANOTHER BLONDE

Although Hollywood insiders knew **JUDY HOLLIDAY** to be a shrewd and intelligent woman, it was well hidden behind the scatter-brained parts she played in the movies. Holliday understood her persona, and when she was called to Washington to testify during the Communist witch hunts, she pretended to be as dumb as the characters she played. Her male questioners fell for it, and she left without giving them a single piece of useful information.

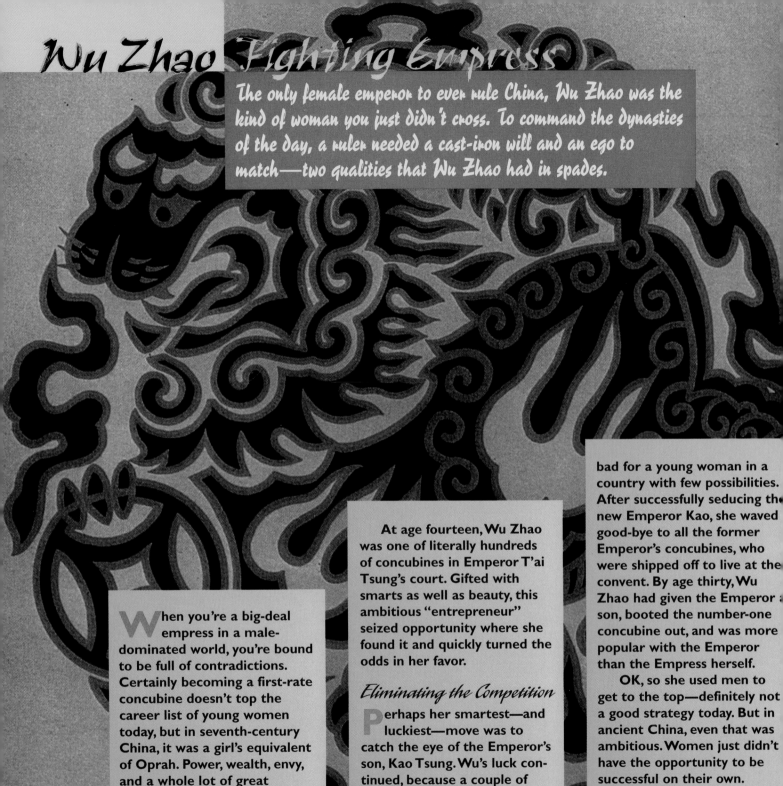

Wu Zhao *Fighting Empress*

The only female emperor to ever rule China, Wu Zhao was the kind of woman you just didn't cross. To command the dynasties of the day, a ruler needed a cast-iron will and an ego to match—two qualities that Wu Zhao had in spades.

When you're a big-deal empress in a male-dominated world, you're bound to be full of contradictions. Certainly becoming a first-rate concubine doesn't top the career list of young women today, but in seventh-century China, it was a girl's equivalent of Oprah. Power, wealth, envy, and a whole lot of great clothes were the reward for catching a powerful man's eye.

At age fourteen, Wu Zhao was one of literally hundreds of concubines in Emperor T'ai Tsung's court. Gifted with smarts as well as beauty, this ambitious "entrepreneur" seized opportunity where she found it and quickly turned the odds in her favor.

Eliminating the Competition

Perhaps her smartest—and luckiest—move was to catch the eye of the Emperor's son, Kao Tsung. Wu's luck continued, because a couple of years later the Emperor died, leaving his son in charge. Not bad for a young woman in a country with few possibilities. After successfully seducing the new Emperor Kao, she waved good-bye to all the former Emperor's concubines, who were shipped off to live at the convent. By age thirty, Wu Zhao had given the Emperor a son, booted the number-one concubine out, and was more popular with the Emperor than the Empress herself.

OK, so she used men to get to the top—definitely not a good strategy today. But in ancient China, even that was ambitious. Women just didn't have the opportunity to be successful on their own. Instead, Wu made the best of her circumstances and forever

Feminism, Feudal Style

Wu Zhao even initiated her own version of women's lib. She did her best to raise the status of women in her culture by commissioning works about important female leaders, and tried to shift the boys-only power structure by promoting a more matriarchal-focused dynasty.

carved a name for herself in Chinese—and international—history.

How'd She Do It?

Well, it wasn't that hard for our intrepid concubine. She was so thoroughly hated by the Empress and the former number-one concubine that they schemed against her. This made it easier to whisper in the Emperor's ear and have her opponents jailed—and quietly killed. Of course, part of the reason the Empress hated Wu Zhao so much was that she shamelessly pointed out how she'd given the Emperor a child—and the Empress hadn't. With her enemies out of the way, Wu made empress by her thirty-first birthday.

So She Wasn't an Angel

Wu Zhao didn't believe in talking through her problems. If anyone got in her way, she simply orchestrated another of her famous "disappearances" which covered pretty much everyone from household help to family members.

Finally the Throne

In 660, her very loving—but not too smart—husband was struck with polio. In moments, Wu Zhao put herself into the imperial chair and went head to head with Korea. Ordering an invasion by sea, she soon annexed the place to

China. Merciless as she sounds, Wu knew how to rule. Her initial severity gave China decades of peace. Her rule yielded plenty of crowd-pleasing results: improved government, new hospitals, health care for the mentally ill, new buildings in the capital, and that old favorite, lower taxes. Despite her more ruthless character quirks, Zhao's legacy to China was one of tranquillity, T'ang art, poetry, and culture.

WHAT ABOUT THOSE BOUND FEET?

Although women weren't exactly liberated in Madame Wu's day, it was a relatively unencumbered time to be a girl in Chinese history. Daughters born into affluent families were schooled in the arts, and allowed to pursue their cultural interests—like painting, literature, and music. And they still got around just fine, thank you, since no one had come up with the half-witted idea of binding their feet.

Courage is the price that life exacts for granting peace.

The soul that knows it not, knows no release

From little things;

Knows not the livid loneliness of fear,

Nor mountain heights where bitter joy can hear

The sound of wings.

Selected Resources

The 100 Most Influential Women of All Time
A Ranking Past and Present
Deborah G. Felder
Citadel Press, 1996

Annie Oakley of the Wild West
Walter Havighurst
Bison Book/Macmillan Publishing, 1992

Amelia: The Centennial Biography of an Aviation Pioneer
Donald M. Goldstein, Katherine V. Dillon
Brasseys Inc., 1997

The American Women's Almanac
Louise Bernikow
Berkley Publishing Group, 1997

Babe: The Life and Legend of Babe Didrikson Zaharias
Susan E. Cayleff
University of Illinois Press, 1996

The Book of Women's Firsts
Phyllis J. Read and Bernard L. Witlieb
Random House, 1992

A Century of Women Cartoonists
Trina Robbins
Kitchen Sink Press, 1993

The Cowgirl Companion
Gail Gilchriest
Hyperion, 1993

Daughters of the Earth
The Lives and Legends of American Indian Women
Carolyn Niethammer
Touchstone/Simon and Schuster, 1977

Desert Queen
The Extraordinary Life of Gertrude Bell: Adventurer, Adviser to Kings, Ally of Lawrence of Arabia
Janet Wallach
Doubleday, 1996

The Encyclopedia of Amazons
Jessica Amanda Salmonson
Anchor Books, Doubleday, 1991

Eva Perón
Nicholas Fraser and Marysa Navarro
Norton, 1980

From Pocahontas to Power Suits
Kay Mills
Penguin Books, 1995

Getting the Real Story
Nellie Bly and Ida B. Wells
Sue Davidson
Seal Press, 1992

The Guinness Book of Espionage
Mark Lloyd
Guinness Publishing Ltd., 1994

Heroines
Norma Lorre Goodrich, HarperPerennial, 1994

A History of Women
Toward a Cultural Identity in the Twentieth Century
Francoise Thebaud, Editor
Belknap Press Harvard University Press, 1994

The I Love Lucy Book
Bart Andrews
Dolphin/Doubleday & Co., 1977

Jump at De Sun: The Story of Zora Neale Hurston
A. P. Porter
First Avenue, 1992

Latin American Heroes
Liberators and Patriots from 1500 to Present
Jerome R. Adams
One World Book, Ballantine, 1991

Madame Curie: A Biography
Eve Curie
De Capo Press, 1986

Maria Callas
Arianna Stassinopoulas
Ballantine, 1982

Mythologies of the Ancient World
Samuel Noah Kramer
Anchor Books, 1961

Night Witches: The Amazing Story of Russia's Women Pilots in World War II
Bruce Myles
Academy Chicago Publisher, 1990

Paris Was a Woman
Portraits from the Left Bank
Andrea Weiss
HarperCollins, 1995

Spies: The Secret Agents Who Changed the Course of History
Ernest Volkman
John Wiley & Sons, 1994

Timelines of American Women's History
Sue Heinemann
Berkley Publishing Group, Roundtable Press, 1996

The Vinland Sagas
The Norse Discovery of America
Magnus Magnusson, Hermann Palsson
Penguin Group, 1965

The Warrior Queens
Antonia Fraser
Vintage Books/Random House, 1988

Without Lying Down: Frances Marion and the Powerful Women of Early Hollywood
Cari Beauchamp, Lisa Drew
Scribner, 1997

Women in Ancient Africa
Heinrich Loth
Lawrence Hill and Company, 1987

Women of the Apache Nation
Voices of Truth
H. Henrietta Stockel
University of Nevada Press, 1993

Women in the Middle Ages
Frances and Joseph Gies
HarperPerennial, 1978

Women in the Viking Age
Judith Jesch
Boydell Press, 1991

Credits

Cover
Joan of Arc: Library of Congress
Mary Pickford: Museum of Modern Art Film Stills
    Archives, New York
Margaret Bourke-White: UPI/Corbis-Bettman
Bessie Smith: Frank Driggs/Corbis-Bettman

p iv–v University of Newcastle upon Tyne

Amazons
p. 2 Bottom right Library of Congress
p. 3 Copyright © 1998 By Universal City Studios, Inc.
    Courtesy of Universal Studios Publishing Rights.
    All Rights Reserved.

Josephine Baker
p. 4 Library of Congress

Lucille Ball
p. 6 Left, bottom, and top right: CBS Photo Archive,
    Desilu, too, LLC
p. 7 Courtesy Desilu, too, LLC

Baseball Barnstormers
p. 8 Top left: National Baseball Hall of Fame Library
    Cooperstown, N.Y.
    Bottom right: UPI/Corbis-Bettman
p. 9 National Baseball Hall of Fame Library
    Cooperstown, N.Y.

Gertrude Bell
pp. 10–11 University of Newcastle upon Tyne

Blues Divas
pp. 12–13 Frank Driggs/Corbis-Bettman

Nellie Bly
p. 14 Corbis-Bettman

Margaret Bourke-White
p. 16 UPI/Corbis-Bettman
p. 17 Library of Congress

Calamity Jane
pp. 18–19 Library of Congress

Maria Callas
p. 21 UPI/Corbis-Bettman

Cleopatra
pp. 22–23 Courtesy The Silents Majority Collection

Madame Curie
pp. 26–27 Library of Congress

Babe Didrikson
p. 28 UPI/Corbis-Bettman
p. 29 Library of Congress

Nancy Drew
pp. 30–31 NANCY DREW is a trademark of Simon &
    Schuster Inc., registered in the United States
    Patent and Trademark Office. Used by permission
    of Simon & Schuster Inc. The jacket art and
    Nancy Drew images are copyrighted by Simon &
    Schuster Inc. and reprinted with permission of
    Pocket Books, a division of Simon & Schuster Inc.

Amelia Earhart
pp. 32–33 U. S. National Archives

Evita Perón
p. 34 UPI/Corbis-Bettman

Janet Flanner
p. 36 Top left and bottom right: Library of Congress
p. 37 (Sylvia Beach) UPI/Corbis-Bettman

Althea Gibson
p. 38 Library of Congress

Cool Goddesses
p. 40 UPI/Corbis-Bettman
p. 41 Middle left: Corbis-Bettman
    Top right: Corbis-Bettman

Jane Goodall
p. 42 UPI/Corbis-Bettman
p. 43 Courtesy of Michael Nichols

Martha Graham
p. 44 Library of Congress
p. 45 (Ruth St. Denis) Library of Congress

Harlem Renaissance
p. 46 Schomberg Center for Research in Black Culture

Hollywood Power Players
pp. 48–49 Museum of Modern Art Film Stills
    Archives, New York

Isabella of Castille
p. 50 Library of Congress

Joan of Arc
pp. 52–53 Library of Congress

Lakshmi Bai, Rani of Jhansi
p. 54 Watercolor from Kalighat, India
    Victoria & Albert Museum, London/Art
    Resource, NY

Lozen, Apache Warrior
p. 56 Arizona Historical Society, Tuscon, AZ

Mother Jones
p. 58 Corbis-Bettman

Shirley Muldowney
pp. 60–61 Courtesy Shirley Muldowney. Jon Asher,
    photographer

Queen Njinga
p. 62 School of Oriental and African Studies,
    University of London

Annie Oakley
p.64–65 The Annie Oakley Foundation Collection

Scarlett O'Hara
p. 66 Turner Entertainment Co.

Georgia O'Keeffe
p. 68 Library of Congress
p. 69 UPI/Corbis-Bettman

Dorothy Parker
p. 70 Corbis-Bettman

Lady Pirates
pp. 72–73 Illustrations by John Kachik

Righteous Queens
p. 74 Turner Entertainment Co.

Rosie the Riveter
pp. 76–77 U. S. National Archives

Margaret Sanger
p. 80 U. S. National Archives
p. 81 Bottom: U. S. National Archives
    Top left: Library of Congress

Soldaderas
p. 82 Courtesy Bazar de Fotografia Casasola

Soviet Flying Aces
p. 84 UPI/Corbis-Bettman

Lady Spies
p. 87 Top left: Corbis-Bettman
    Bottom right: U. S. National Archives

Suffragists
pp. 88–89 Library of Congress

Harriet Tubman
p. 90 Library of Congress

Viking Women
p. 93 "The Valkyrie" oil painting by John Gruse, courtesy
    John Gruse

Madame C.J. Walker
pp. 94–95 Schomberg Center for Research in Black Culture

W.A.S.P.s
p. 96 Courtesy Alice Stevens Rohrer
p. 97 Bottom left: Courtesy Dorothy Mann Britt
    Top right: Courtesy Alice Stevens Rohrer

Mae West
p. 98 Roger Richman Agency
p. 99 Top: Roger Richman Agency
    Bottom right (Judy Holiday): Library of Congress

p. 102 U. S. National Archives

ILLUSTRATIONS
pp 2, 57, 78–79 from *Women*, selected by Jim Harter, Dover
    Publications Inc., New York
p 75 from *Perspective*, Jan Vredeman de Vries, Dover
    Publications Inc., New York
pp. 100–101 from *Full-Color Designs from Chinese Opera
    Costumes*, edited by the Northeast Drama Institute,
    Dover Publications Inc., New York